# CACTI

by
FRANK D. VENNING

Illustrated by
MANABU C. SAITO

 GOLDEN PRESS • NEW YORK
Western Publishing Company, Inc.
Racine, Wisconsin

# FOREWORD

Of all the plants in the world, few are more remarkable than cacti for their strange forms, spectacular flowers, and amazing adaptations for survival. Originating as small leafy jungle trees, they first adapted over the aeons to life in the desert. But during further ages many again adapted to other conditions, so that modern cacti are by no means all desert dwellers.

Some species became tolerant to cold, and now grow in grasslands on the plains and prairies, or live high up in the mountains, even far above the timberline. Others now prefer the seacoast, while still others have returned to the jungle, where they take the form of scrambling vines, or cling as air-plants high in the forest trees. Yet within all these diverse habitats, most cacti are highly adapted to occupy special ecological niches in the environment—niches where they can avoid competition by living under conditions so difficult or unusual that few other plants can survive or prosper there.

This book surveys the Cactus Family by illustrating and describing selected species and varieties to show the range of form and adaptation within it, and includes many species and varieties native to the United States.

F. D. V.

# CONTENTS

# THE ORIGIN OF CACTI

Cacti originated in the Americas, most probably in Mexico, but now range from British Columbia to Massachusetts, and all the way down to Patagonia, near the tip of South America. Our knowledge of their history is incomplete, because few cacti ever inhabited sites where fossil formation could occur; studies of continental drift and climatic changes during geologic times give some insight into their development:

Before the rise of flowering plants, when cone-bearing trees dominated the earth, all of the land was united as a single super-continent with a warm moist climate, surrounded by a single ocean. Then, about 135 million years ago, as dinosaurs declined and the insects arose, flowering plants began to compete with the conifers; at the same time, rifts appeared in the earth's crust. The northern and southern land-mass split apart, and a rift also appeared between Africa and South America. North America split from Europe 80 million years ago, and also began drifting west.

By 65 million years ago, the North and South Atlantic Oceans had taken shape, South America and Africa were 2000 miles apart, flowering plants dominated the landscape, and the universal warm moist climate ended. Broad bands of dry climate gradually appeared on each side of the 30th parallel in the northern and southern hemispheres, and the stage was set for the cacti to appear. But apparently all the ancestral prototypes were isolated in the Americas, or evolved there after the continents had drifted apart.

It is thought that the ancestors of the highly specialized modern cacti were small leafy trees with a woody trunk, not too different from some present-day Pereskias

(Pages 10-11). These are mostly drought-avoiding plants; they simply shed their leaves and go dormant during the dry season. Others have slightly thickened leaves that store small reserves of water.

Only two fossil cacti have ever been found. The oldest, from Utah, lived about 50 million years ago in the Middle Eocene. It was a flat-jointed plant much like a prickly pear but with more primitive fruits, confirming that some cacti were specialized for life in an arid environment that long ago. The other fossil, from Arizona, is of a recent Opuntia from the Pleistocene, less than 2 million years old.

## ADAPTATIONS FOR SURVIVAL

As the American deserts came into being, cacti confronted an environment of intense sunlight, low humidity, hot dry winds, scanty rainfall, and extreme fluctuations between day and night-time temperatures. Survival under these conditions meant resolving two problems: how to handle excessive heat, and how to avoid drying up. Adaptation required the ability to make continual adjustments to prevent internal temperatures from becoming lethal, while losing as little water as possible.

It should be kept in mind that chlorophyll, the pigment necessary for photosynthesis, appears green to the eye because it absorbs much of the blue-violet and short red rays of the spectrum, but reflects most of the green rays; a part of the absorbed radiant energy is converted to heat, causing a plant to heat up inside. During the day, large Opuntias and barrel cacti become $18°$ to $27°$ F hotter than the surrounding air. (Experiments show that some Opuntias can survive internal temperatures approaching $145°$ F, which is above the lethal maximum for many other cacti.)

A basic way in which cacti have adapted is by modifying their forms so as to reduce the amount of external surface in relation to their total volume. This led to abandoning green leaves, transferring photosynthesis to the stem, and the stems becoming more and more globe-like in many species. In addition, cacti developed mechanisms for reducing the heat load.

Prickly pears often position their joints with the flat sides facing east and west; thus the intense midday sunlight only strikes the thin upper edge of the pads. Some developed pigments that reflect part of the red or blue light; others have tiny surface hairs that scatter some of the incoming radiation.

Cactus spines are actually highly modified leaves; beside affording physical protection, they absorb and reflect much light, keeping the underlying tissue as much as 20° F cooler than it would be if they were lacking. The spines, bristles, and hairs that adorn cacti also trap a thin layer of air next to the stem, which acts as insulation and slows heat transfer.

Cacti also have mechanisms for collecting and conserving water. The absorbing roots, mostly in the upper soil, can make fuller use of light rains of slight penetration. Many young cacti have down-pointing spines that act as drip-tips; these collect fog, dew, or light rain and channel it to the roots. And most cacti have an abundance of water-storage tissue in their stems or roots, with reinforced walls to prevent its collapse when water reserves are low.

The stomates, or pores through which cacti breathe and exchange gases with the air, are sunken in pits below the stem surface, reducing water vapor loss from 30 to 70 percent. Those of cacti can close during the heat of the day, when the transpiration rate would be high.

The cell sap is mucilaginous, and as water reserves are used the protoplasm becomes thick and viscous, binding the dwindling water more and more tightly. And some cacti can maintain a constant water balance by oxidizing their stored sugar. In one experiment, Opuntia joints were kept in the dark for 5 months at 82° F; they maintained a constant internal water balance during the whole time, although they lost water constantly through transpiration.

All these marvelous adaptations for survival in a hostile environment carried a "price tag:" the more specialized a cactus became in handling excessive heat and conserving water, the more its life processes and growth rate were forced to slow down. In turn, the slow rate of growth restricts ability to compete among ordinary faster-growing leafy plants in a more moist environment. And some cacti have become so highly adapted to a specific habitat that if even a slight change were to occur in the environment, they would probably face extinction.

## ABERRANT FORMS OF CACTI

In cacti that grow as columns or globes, each stem has a single delicate growing point at the tip, usually within a slight depression, and protected by a mass of felt, wool, and spines. But occasionally the growing point is injured and its cells begin dividing asymmetrically; the new growth takes monstrous forms or twists like a corkscrew. The growing point may gradually turn into a growth line, forming crests, fans, or domes at the top of the plant.

Some cactus seedlings are born without chlorophyll. In nature they die while tiny, after consuming the food stored in the seed. But they live and grow indefinitely if grafted onto a green cactus rootstock.

# CLASSIFICATION OF CACTI

When the Conquistadors landed in the Americas, they were astonished by the cacti. Examples sent to Europe amazed botanists and laymen alike, and truly seemed to be plants from a New World. Their spines suggested they were somehow like thistles; when Linnaeus founded the present system of plant classification in 1753, he grouped them under the name Cactus, from the ancient Greek word *kaktos,* meaning thistle. Ever since, this plant family has been the *Cactaceae,* a single plant a *cactus,* more than one plant *cacti.* They are not too closely related to any other family, and are placed in a separate Order, *Cactales,* within the Class *Dicotyledonae* (the flowering plants whose seeds have two cotyledons, or seed leaves).

In addition to naming plants, classification forms a framework upon which all other knowledge of plants is arranged so it can be readily found when needed. To provide a usable framework, plants must be grouped to show the natural relationships between them. And within each family, classification should conform with prevailing practice throughout the world as a whole for naming the entire Plant Kingdom.

During the first half of this century, radical systems of cactus classification were published, creating vast numbers of new genera and species, many based on trivial or unstable characteristics, thus obscuring natural relationships within the family. Today, cacti are receiving painstaking study and careful revisions in classification. The scientific names of cacti used in this book agree with the conservative revisions that have thus far been made in the family. As additional revisions occur, notations to that effect will be included.

# GLOSSARY

**Acute,** terminating in a sharp or well-defined angle.

**Annulate,** made up of horizontal ring-like bands.

**Apex,** the tip or summit of a structure.

**Areole,** in cacti, a clearly defined small area that may bear felt, hair, spines, glochids, flowers, or new branches.

**Axil,** the upper angle that a structure makes with the stem to which it is attached.

**Cephalium,** a permanent head with a woody core that develops at the stem apex when a plant is mature; bears the flowers and fruits.

**Coalesce,** to grow together.

**Corymb,** a short broad flower-cluster in which the lower flowers open first.

**Deciduous,** falling off at maturity, or at certain seasons.

**Diurnal,** day-blooming.

**Epiphyte,** growing on other plants, but not parasitic.

**Glaucous,** covered by a whitish "bloom" that rubs off.

**Glochid,** a thin barbed bristle, produced in the areoles of Chollas, Prickly Pears, and a few other cacti.

**Monotypic,** having one species.

**Nocturnal,** night-blooming.

**Offshoot,** a new plant arising from the mother plant.

**Ovary,** the lower swollen part of the pistil, containing ovules; after fertilization, the ovules develop into seeds and the ovary into the fruit.

**Panicle,** a simple elongate cluster of flowers, the lower-most opening first.

**Perianth,** the sepals and petals collectively; said of cactus flowers where there is a gradual transition from sepal-like to petal-like parts.

**Persistent,** remaining attached.

**Pistil,** the female part of the flower; the *ovary* at its base becomes the fruit, the *stigma* at its tip is the pollen receiver, which the tubular *style* connects to the ovary.

**Porrect,** standing perpendicular to the surface.

**Pseudocephalium,** a "false head," a temporary modification of the stem at flowering; it does not prevent further growth of the green stem, as does a *cephalium*.

**Scale,** a small vestigial leaf.

**Scrub,** a region of low, often dense stunted bushes.

**Sepal,** one of the outer segments of the perianth.

**Stamen,** the pollen-bearing (male) part of the flower.

**Stigma,** the pollen-receiver at the tip of the style.

**Stolon,** a horizontal stem at or below ground that produces a new plant at its tip.

**Style,** elongate connection between the ovary and stigma.

**Tuber,** underground stem used as a storage organ.

**Tubercle,** a nipple-like protrusion from stem or fruit.

**Zygomorphic,** bilaterally symmetrical.

**PERESKIA**, a Tropical American genus of leafy trees, shrubs, and vines, more closely resembles ordinary woody plants rather than cacti. Pereskias are living examples of nonsucculent primitive cacti from which the succulent species evolved. They have sharp smooth unsheathed spines on the trunk, branches, and in the leaf axils. Leaves are alternate, broad, flat, deciduous or rather fleshy; flowers are solitary or in corymbs or panicles. The edible fruits can be leafy.

Most Pereskias root easily from cuttings and are often used as living fenceposts or for hedges, and as rootstocks for grafting ornamental epiphytic cacti.

**PERESKIA GUAMACHO,** Guamacho, a little tree up to 16 feet high, is common along the semi-arid Caribbean coast of Colombia and Venezuela. The bark of trunk and branches is yellowish-green, on which the old areoles stand out like small knobs filled with brown felt and rigid spines. In the dry season the leaves are dropped; the tree flowers profusely before refoliating. The flowers close at night, opening again the next morning at 9 am. The trunk, up to 15 inches in diameter, is used for wood.

**P. ACULEATA** (prickly), Barbados Gooseberry, Lemon Vine, or Blade Apple, begins life as an erect shrub, but later grows clambering branches over 30 feet long that scale rocks, walls, and trees. The showy lemon-scented blossoms are followed by clusters of yellow berries eaten throughout the West Indies; the leaves are cooked as a pot herb in Brazil. There are also white and yellow-flowered races. Long in cultivation, this species was grown at the Royal Gardens at Hampton Court before 1696.

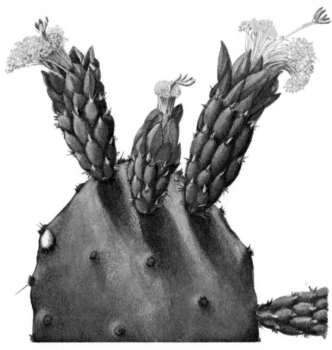

**NOPALEA**, closely related to Opuntia, differs in that the sepals and petals do not open, but remain upright and closely appressed around the numerous stamens and the style, which are much longer than the petals.

**N. COCHINELLIFERA**, the Cochineal Cactus, had long been grown in "nopalries" by the Aztecs before Cortez conquered Mexico in 1518. Small cottony-white patches on the joints were brushed off, crushed, and steamed, releasing the scarlet dye Cochineal. The Crown ordered all that could be obtained, and plantings were made in the Old and New Worlds. Only in 1703, by aid of a microscope, were the white growths found to be insects (females of Coccus cacti scale), not part of Nopalea itself. The industry waned after the discovery of aniline dyes; now revived in the Canaries.

**OPUNTIA** (Cholla; Prickly Pear) is native to much of the Western Hemisphere, ranging from Massachusetts to British Columbia, and southward to the Straits of Magellan. Individual species vary from 20-foot trees with spreading crowns to small ground-hugging plants a few inches high.

The stems and branches are chains of ribless joints that are globular, cylindrical, or flattened, usually very fleshy, but sometimes woody. If tubercles are present they are separate, not fused together, with the areole uppermost. Areoles are rather uniformly distributed over the flat-sided species.

On new growth, a leaf develops just beneath each areole; these leaves are usually small fleshy awl-like appendages from ¼ to 1 inch long, rarely to 2 inches, that are quickly shed as the joint matures. Areoles are commonly armed with from 1 to 15 or 20 spines that emerge from the lower side of the areole; a few species are spineless. The spines vary greatly in color, length, and texture; mostly they are smooth, but sculptured or barbed in a few. The areoles of all Opuntias are armed with tufts of glochids: tiny barbed bristles, easily detached, that readily penetrate the skin and work their way into the flesh.

Flower-buds appear from within the areoles located near the top of joints grown during the previous season. Flowers are diurnal and may last several days. The tube is very short above its connection to the ovary, with the stamens attached to this part of the tube; it is deciduous after flowering.

The ripe fruits are either fleshy or dry; they are often bright-colored and long-lasting, making some species more attractive when in fruit than when in flower. Their areoles may be hairy or spiny.

**OPUNTIA ECHINOCARPA** (spiny-fruited) Silver or Golden Cholla is an intricately-branched shrub or dwarf tree of gravelly or sandy soils of the Sonoran, Mojave, and Colorado Deserts between 1000 and 5600 feet elevation. It ranges from NE Baja California and W Sonora, Mexico, across SE California, S Nevada, SW Utah, and W Arizona.

Its branches, like those of all Chollas, are tuberculate and circular in cross-section. The dense awl-shaped spines, 3 to 12 per areole, are straight and unbarbed, ¾ to 1½ inches long. Individual plants are either silver or golden-spined. As in all Chollas, the epidermis of each spine separates into a thin papery sheath; sheaths are conspicuous and persistent, the same color as the spine.

Flowering in mid-spring, the dry tan deciduous fruits ripen in early summer.

**O. SPINOSIOR** (full of spines), Cane Cholla, prefers deep soils of desert grasslands at 2000 to 6500 feet elevation. From Sonora and Chihuahua, Mexico, it ranges north into SE Arizona and SW New Mexico.

A little tree with a short thick trunk and long branches, rendered conspicuous by whorls of short joints at right angles to the main branches and its gray or purplish-gray spines. The joints, mostly 5 to 12 inches long and about an inch thick, are studded by small tubercles. The short barbed spines, 10 to 20 per areole, have dull tan sheaths. The lacy wooden inner core of the stems is prized for making canes.

The 2-inch flowers appear in spring; their color varies between plants, from purple and red to yellow, green, or rarely white. The strongly-tuberculate fleshy oval fruits are yellow, spineless, 1¾ inches long.

15

**OPUNTIA IMBRICATA** (overlapping, referring to the appearance of the tubercles) Coyonostle; Tree Cholla, grows at elevations of 4000 to 6000 feet, preferring sandy or gravelly soils of the grasslands. It is found mostly E of the Rockies, from central Mexico to SE Colorado and SW Kansas, including W Oklahoma and the W half of Texas.

Tree Chollas have cylindrical joints 5 to 15 inches long and about an inch thick, with very prominent sharply-raised tubercles. The strongly-barbed spines, 10 to 30 per areole and ½ to 1⅛ inches long, are almost needle-like but slightly flattened, with dull tan papery sheaths that last about a year.

The flowers, 2 to 3 inches wide, appear in late spring. The yellow spineless fruits, to 1¾ inches long, are fleshy, strongly tuberculate; they hold through winter.

16

**O. VERSICOLOR** (variously colored, referring to the flowers) called Staghorn Cholla, grows in deep sandy soils of canyons, valleys, and washes of the Arizona Desert in N Sonora and south-central Arizona. Adult plants are small trees, the ultimate branches reminiscent of a stag's antlers.

The joints, mostly 5 to 14 inches long and less than 1 inch thick, have fairly prominent long tubercles. The spines, 7 to 10 per areole, are short, slightly barbed, and lose their sheaths within a month or two.

The flowers, 1¼ to 2¼ inches wide, appear in spring; each plant has its own color, varying from purple, red, and rose to yellow, orange, bronze, brown, or green. The branches tend to take the same color as the flowers in winter or during drought. The fruits persist for several years; new fruits sometimes develop from the old.

17

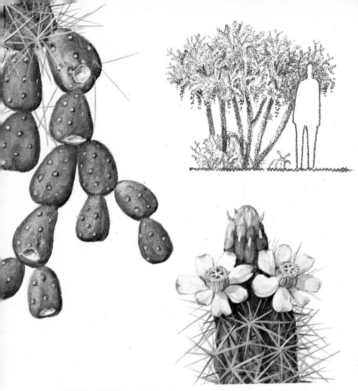

**OPUNTIA FULGIDA** (glistening, referring to the spines) called Jumping Cholla, often forms forests on sandy desert soils at 1000 to 3000 feet elevation. Ranges from Sinaloa, Mexico, northward to central Arizona.

The joints, 2 to 6 inches long and to 2 inches thick, with large mammillate tubercles, are almost hidden behind the dense barbed spines. A puff of wind, or the vibration of a footstep will detach the terminal joints, which quickly root and propagate the plant. If touched or dropped on man or animal, the flesh is pierced.

Flowering extends from early spring to September. The juicy fruits, usually spineless, are held on the plant and sought by grazing animals. The areoles of old fruits bear flowers, in turn forming new fruits linked to the old.

**O. BIGELOVII** (for Jacob M. Bigelow, 1786-1879, American botanist) called Teddy Bear Cholla; Ball Cholla, has vicious strongly barbed spines, very hard to remove from skin or flesh. Its joints "jump" at a bare touch.

This cholla grows in rocky or gravelly soils, from Sonora and N Baja California, Mexico, north over the Colorado Desert and lower Arizona Desert, in SE California and W and S Arizona, at elevations of 100 to 3000 feet. On mountain slopes or hills, it grows on the warm sunny southern side.

Branches of these miniature trees are much shorter than the central trunk. The ultimate joints are 3-inch spheres.

The tiny round fleshy fruits, less than an inch wide, are hidden by the spines of the joints; last for one winter.

19

**OPUNTIA LEPTOCAULIS** (with thin stems) also called Desert Christmas Cactus, Tasajillo, and Tesajo, usually grows among the desert scrub on plains and bottomlands at elevations of 200 to 3000 feet. It ranges widely, from Puebla, Mexico, to W-central Arizona, east to SW and S-central Oklahoma, and over W and S Texas.

This trunkless cholla is a bush or erect small shrub, the main branches composed of thin cylindrical joints to 16 inches long, with dense woody cores. Tubercles are obscure, and the joints are smooth. Each areole produces just one needle-like slightly barbed spine 1 to 2 inches long. Lateral joints are only 1 to 3 inches long, less than ¼-inch thick, at first spineless.

Flower color varies from yellow to green or bronze. The fruits hold over winter; conspicuous when the desert is drab.

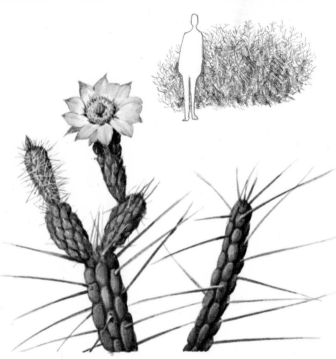

**O. RAMOSISSIMA** (much-branched) also called Diamond Cholla, grows in sandy desert washes and on the desert floor at 100 to as much as 3000 feet elevation, from NW Sonora to the S Mojave and Colorado Deserts, S California, S Nevada, and W Arizona.

Either shrubby, matted, or tree-like, the main branches much rebranched, this cholla is among the least succulent; the inner core of young shoots be-comes wood within a year.

The joints are 2 to 4 inches long and ¼-inch thick, covered by flat diamond-shaped tuber-cles with areoles in notches at the upper ends. Spines cluster 1 to 4 per areole, but only 1 develops, from 1½ to 2¼ inches long, with many barbs and a thin conspicuous sheath.

Flowers are borne on short lateral branches. The many stamens give them a yellow hue; actual petal color varies.

**OPUNTIA ERINACEA** (like a hedgehog) var. ursina (bear-like), known as Grizzly Bear Cactus, grows on rocky hillsides in the Mojave Desert at 4000 to 5500 feet elevation, in N Arizona, SW Utah, S Nevada and SE California.

This flat-jointed prickly pear is notable for long tawny-white flexible spines that cover the bases of the lower joints. Some of these spines are 3 or 4 inches long in wild plants; in fine cultivated selections they are more than twice this length. The joints themselves are elongated, 4 to 5 inches long and 1 to 2 inches wide.

The plants form clumps a foot high and a yard or more wide; as one nears a slope where it is growing, the hillside appears to be covered by patches of snow.

The brownish-tan fruits, dry when ripe, are densely spined and deciduous.

**O. RUFIDA** (reddish-brown, referring to the glochids) also known as Blind Prickly Pear inhabits rocky desert hillsides and ridges at elevations of 1900 to 3360 feet in the States of Chihuahua and Coahuila, Mexico, and the Big Bend region of Texas. It seldom grows more than 20 miles north of the Rio Grande.

This 6-foot shrub develops a definite trunk, and has large round flat joints from 3 to 10 inches across. Their color varies from blue-green to gray-green, and their surface is rendered dull by a covering of hair.

The spineless areoles are large and close together, filled by a conspicuous hemispherical tuft of short slender glochids that are easily detached. Grazing cattle relish feeding on the joints and the small fleshy bright red fruit of this cactus; the glochids readily penetrate the eye and blind them.

23

**OPUNTIA BASILARIS** (pertaining to the base, referring to the low spreading habit of branching) known as Beaver-Tail Cactus grows on sandy, gravelly, or rocky soils in or near the desert, mostly between sea level and 4000 feet, rarely to 9000 feet elevation. It ranges over N Sonora and S California to S Nevada, S Utah, and W Arizona.

The Beaver-Tail is a variable species that forms clumps only 6 to 12 inches high but up to 2 yards across. Typically, the form of the spineless joints is suggestive of a beaver's tail. The surface is velvety, the areoles conspicuous and depressed, full of troublesome glochids.

At maturity the 1-inch fruits are dry, tan or light gray, full of nearly circular bone-white or pale gray seeds.

Var. *treleasei* is armed with spines on joints and fruit; var. *aurea* is yellow-flowered.

24

**O. VIOLACEA** var. **santa rita** (for the Santa Rita Mountains near Tucson, Arizona, in the vicinity of which it was discovered) Purple Prickly Pear, one of the most ornamental of the Opuntias, develops a trunk and sometimes becomes large and tree-like. It grows in sandy or gravelly soils in N Sonora, S Arizona, S New Mexico, and in Texas W of the Pecos River, at elevations of 3000 to 5000 feet, at the desert's edge.

The nearly circular joints, 6 to 8 inches wide, are usually spineless. A few needle-like spines, 1 per areole, may occur on the upper margin of the pad, these are from 1½ to 2½ inches long.

The red or reddish-purple fleshy fruits are oval, to 1½ inches long.

This cactus lives within narrow environmental limits, and is not tolerant of drought or of too much moisture.

**OPUNTIA MACRORHIZA** (large roots) Plains Prickly Pear, a clump-forming species usually only 3 to 5 inches high but the clumps to 6 feet wide, is common on the Great Plains grasslands and the high plains of the West at elevations of 2000 to 8000 feet, from E California to South Dakota. Although rare on the prairies, it occurs eastward to S Michigan, W Ohio, W Missouri, W Arkansas, and Louisiana, central and S Texas and occurs across most of the northern part of Mexico.

The main root or roots are tuberous, but the roots put down by the prostrate joints are fibrous. The joints are 2 to 4 inches long and 2 to 3 inches wide. Most of the spines come from the upper areoles, 1 to 6 per areole, needle-like up to 2¼ inches long.

The purple or purplish-red fruits, to 1½ inches long, are fleshy and bear glochids.

**O. FICUS-INDICA**, Indian Fig; Nopal de Castilla, thought to be native to Mexico, is found all over the tropics and very mild-temperate parts of the world. It has long been grown for its fruits and for forage.

The plants are tree-like, to over 15 feet high, with a foot-thick trunk 2 to 4 feet long. The fleshy oblong joints, 1 to 2 feet long and 8 to 16 inches wide, may have no, a few, or many spines, depending on which of the many horticultural varieties or hybrids is involved. All have numerous glochids, that drop off as the joint ages.

It has escaped and runs wild along the Mediterranean, the Red Sea, and in Mexico and Hawaii; it has become a noxious weed in South Africa and particularly in Australia, where cattle, sheep, emus, and other animals eat the fruit and spread seed to over 1,000,000 new uninfested acres each year.

27

**CEREUS,** as interpreted by modern taxonomists, contains an undetermined but large number of species ranging from California, Arizona, New Mexico, Texas, and Florida southward into Chile and Argentina; sixteen species are native or introduced and established as a part of the flora of the United States.

Cereus is characterized by elongated ribbed stems which branch slightly to freely. Mature stems are from 15 to 100 times as long as their diameter, i.e., from 1 to 50 feet long, and from ¼ inch to 2½ feet in diameter. Ribs vary from 3 to more than 20, so that in cross-section the stems have prismatic to cylindrical outlines. The stems expand and contract as water is absorbed, stored, and used. Leaves are not produced on the new growth of mature stems, but do occur on seedling Cereus.

The smooth straight needle-like spines, from 1 to many per areole, are usually between 1/16 of an inch to 3 inches long, but a few species have 8- to 10-inch spines, the largest in the Cactus Family.

Flowers are produced on the old growth of preceding seasons, and therefore are below the growing apex of the stem or branch. Buds develop in felted areas at least within the edge of the spine-bearing part of the areoles, or merge into it. Most species have showy flowers, but they vary greatly in size; the majority are from 1 to 6 inches wide when fully open, but some have flowers a foot long and equally wide. In form the flowers are essentially tubular, but the part above the ovary is almost tubeless in some, funnel-form in others, long and trumpet-like in a few.

At maturity the fruit is fleshy and often edible. Its skin may be with or without tubercles, scales, hairs, spines, or a combination of these.

28

**C. NUDIFLORUS** (naked-flowered) Flor de Copa (Goblet-Flower) is the most tree-like Cereus. Old plants develop a thick upright cylindrical trunk with a solid wood core, sheathed by fine-grained grayish-brown bark, with dense clusters of sharp rigid spines in the areoles. With age some areoles develop into rounded knobs protruding from the bark.

The much-branched spreading crown reaches a height of over 30 feet and is usually as broad as the plant is tall. The branches are made up of numerous joints with 3 to 5 wings, a slender woody core, and low scallops on the wing margins.

The birch-scented flowers are nocturnal. The fruits resemble avocados, and are the largest Cactus fruits known.

This species is common on the coasts of Cuba and Hispaniola, from Havana Province eastward.

29

**CEREUS JAMACARU**, Manda-carú, is native to the notorious "dry polygon" of northeastern Brazil, where it often dominates the landscape along the coast and in the arid interior. Boards cut from its woody trunk are made into boxes, crates, and picture frames. The country people use the wood as cross-pieces on which to lay the roof tiles.

The dense compact crown of upright branches reaches 30

feet in height. Branches have 4 to 6 ribs; when young the ribs are thin, high, very blue in color, with wavy margins. Old stems and branches are covered with spines up to 8 inches long. The nocturnal flowers, each a foot long, are borne in profusion; the bright red oval fruits are esteemed.

The farmers plant Manda-carú in hedges, and in times of drought cut the branches to feed their livestock.

**C. HEXAGONUS** (six-angled) Blue Cereus, native to the southern West Indies and northeastern South America, is much admired and frequently planted in dooryards and parks within its range. Although old plants are tree-like and reported to reach almost 50 feet, average specimens are usually less than half this height, columnar in form, usually branching near the base from a short woody trunk.

The branches, a distinct blue-green, are made up of short ribbed joints about 5 inches thick, often have 6 ribs, but the ribs vary from 4 to 7 on individual joints. Young joints are spineless or carry few very short spines, but old branches bear clusters of unequal spines to 2½ inches long.

The nocturnal flowers, 8 to 10 inches long, cover the plant when it blooms; the pale red oval fruits have edible pulp.

**CEREUS REPANDUS** (with wavy margins, referring to the silouette of the branches) Cadushi, of the arid plains of northwestern Venezuela and the Netherlands Antilles, forms thickets on Curacao, where it is important economically. The strong woody trunk, 12 to 16 inches thick, provides boards for making small decorative tables, chests, and chairs.

The columnar branches reach to 35 feet, are about 4 inches thick, with 9 to 12 ribs which are irregularly constricted and bear areoles set with clusters of spines up to 2½ inches long.

The flesh of the branches is a staple food of Curacao, sold fresh or as dry granular powder. When added to boiling water and cooked, it forms a mucilaginous green soup stock with a mild asparagus flavor.

The flesh is also used as soap; it foams readily and dissolves grease.

**C. PERUVIANUS** (of Peru, a misnomer) Hedge Cactus, is thought to be native to Uruguay, but it has been widely cultivated for such a long time that its origin is in doubt. Typically columnar and upright, densely branched at or near the base, in age it forms a compact crown to nearly 50 feet.

Young branches are 4 inches thick with 6 to 8 flat ribs, a light green, changing to bluish gray in the second season. The tips are covered with brown felt intermixed with longer fluffy strands. Mature limbs are light grayish-green, to 8 inches thick. Needle-like spines to 1⅛ inches long are in clusters of 5 to 10 per areole.

The slightly fragrant nocturnal flowers, 6 inches long, are bell-like, not opening wide. The fruits are partly tubercled.

As is true of most Cereus, branch cuttings root readily and are used for hedges.

33

**CEREUS PECTEN-ABORIGINUM** (aborigine's comb) Indian's Comb; Hairbrush Cactus, a tree-like Mexican species from the States of Chihuahua, Sonora, Colima, and Baja California, forms a woody trunk 3 to 6 feet high and a foot thick.

Branches have 10 or 11 ribs; each rib has a narrow groove running down its outer edge in which the areoles are seated. Flower-producing areoles are filled with dense reddish or brownish wool and develop brownish cushions connected to the areoles below; other areoles are filled with gray wool. Spines are in clusters of 8 to 12, usually short.

The diurnal flowers are only 2 to 3 inches long. The fruit is covered by 5-inch yellow bristles; these dry fruits are used by the native women of Baja California as combs.

34

**C. CHRYSOMALLUS** (golden fleece), native to the states of Puebla and Oaxaca, Mexico, is a characteristic plant on the mesas around Tehuacán. Fully-grown specimens are massive columnar tree-like plants, the 6-foot trunk and older branches stout and woody. Old plants have compact cylindrical crowns over 50 feet high and 16 feet wide, made up of hundreds of erect stems.

The stems are glaucous green in color with 11 to 14 ribs; the areoles are studded along the outer edge of the ribs. There are 12 slender radial and 3 central spines per areole; one of the latter is very long, to over 5 inches.

The nocturnal flowers, borne near the top of the stem, are often hidden in it. The fruits mature and burst open just one month after flowering.

**CEREUS GIGANTEUS** (gigantic) Saguaro, the State Flower of Arizona.

From the headwaters of the Yaqui River in southern Sonora, the Saguaro ranges northward across the Arizona Desert and the upper edge of the Colorado Desert to the beginning of the Colorado Plateau in central Arizona, at elevations of 600 to 3600 feet. This range includes southeastern California near the Colorado River, from the Whipple Mountains to the Laguna Dam.

Large Saguaro forests are common in southern Arizona and Sonora, but the species is by no means continuously distributed throughout its range. It is restricted to rocky or gravelly soils of the hills, canyons, and along desert washes. It seldom occurs on alluvial soils, seemingly because these do not provide adequate anchorage for the plant.

Saguaros lack taproots, and although the lateral roots radiate out for a distance of 50 to 60 feet, they lie only a few inches beneath the soil. Strong winds are common in rainy weather throughout its range, and the rocky soils give better support to the tons of stem swaying in the wind than do rain-softened alluviums.

Although not the largest of cacti (*Cereus pringlei* of Mexico is larger, and the largest cactus known), adult Saguaros are truly gigantic awe-inspiring plants 50 feet high, the trunk 2½ feet thick, the base of the upraised arms curving outward high overhead, the whole cactus weighing 10 tons. This weight is supported by a cylinder of 12 or more woody rods extending up the entire stem, with succulent tissue both to the inside and out. The wood, impregnated with silicon, quickly blunts woodworking tools.

Saguaros grow very slowly. After 2 years, plants are ¼-inch tall; at 15 years, barely 1 foot; by 40 years, not more than 10 feet. At 60 to 70 years and from 2 to 3 times a man's height, the first branch buds appear near the top. Plants usually have 1 to 5 branches and little rebranching. Mature plants are 150 to 200 years old.

In Arizona, flowering is from late April through June; buds are crowded in a wide circle of up to 300 just below the branch tips, but only about a third of them develop fully. Flowers open in late evening and remain open until early afternoon of the next day. Self-sterile, they are pollinated by bees, white-winged doves, and nectar-drinking bats.

The egg-shaped fruits, 2 to 3 inches long, ripen in July; the skin splits and curls back, exposing the vivid red pulp. Papago Indians make a heavy syrup and an intoxicating wine from them; their harvest marks the Papago New Year.

Gila woodpeckers dig nest holes in the soft pulp of the stems; the raw surface callouses and grows corky, making a perfect jug. Pima Indians use these for water-bottles.

**CEREUS GEOMETRIZANS** (symmetric) Padre Nuestro (Our Father), is a common cactus of the Mexican tableland from San Luis Potosi to Oaxaca. Mature plants are tree-like, 15 feet high, with a short definite trunk and much-branched spreading top.

The bluish-green branches, 2 to 4 inches thick, have 5 or 6 rounded ribs with broad intervals. They are glaucous, with a bright bluish-white "bloom" from the waxy cuticle that pro-

tects them; in winter the color deepens to smoky violet. The areoles bear 5 short radial spines and one central dagger-like spine one inch long.

Small myrtle-like diurnal flowers, slightly over an inch wide, appear singly or in two's from the upper part of the areoles. The edible olive-like fruits, called Garambullos, are sold in the Mexican markets; they are eaten fresh, or dried and used in much the same way as are raisins.

**C. LANATUS** (woolly) Peruvian Old Man; Cotton Ball, from the dry Andean uplands of southern Equador and northern Peru, has two distinct growth habits: the plants may be erect columns to 12 feet high, sometimes with a few simple upright branches, or they are treelike, with many 3-foot horizontal branches that curve upward and become erect at the stem tip.

Stems and branches have 20 low rounded ribs bearing rows of rather large areoles spaced ¼-inch apart. The areoles carry large clusters of short needle-like radial spines, and a single central spine up to 2 inches long. The areoles also produce abundant long white hairs, completely hiding the stem tips under a massive growth of wool and spines.

Flowers, produced on one side of the stem from a pseudocephalium, are about 2 inches wide. The small edible fruits are sweet and juicy.

**CEREUS SCHOTTII** (for F. Arthur Schott, plant collector with the Mexican Boundary Survey) Senita, grows in both heavy and sandy soils in Baja California and the Sonoran Deserts at elevations of 1500 feet or less; its natural range crosses the border into western Pima County, Arizona.

Senitas are trunkless, with elongated columnar branches mostly arising from near the base, in age forming colonies from 6 to 21 feet high and up to 15 feet in diameter. Branches are about 5 inches thick, with 5 to 9 prominent ribs.

The areoles of young branches carry clusters of about 8 to 10 short stout spines with bulbous bases, but when branches reach flowering age, each new areole produces a tuft of 30 to 50 twisted bristle-like spines up to 3 inches long.

The small nocturnal flowers emit an evil scent.

**C. THURBERI** (for George Thurber, 1821-1890, botanist with the Mexican Boundary Survey) Organ-Pipe Cactus; Pitahaya, grows at elevations of 1000 to 3500 feet on the rocky and sandy hills, mesas, and valleys in the deserts of Baja California and western Sonora, northward to western Pima and southwestern Pinal Counties, Arizona.

These are large columnar plants 9 to 20 feet high and 6 to 18 feet in diameter, with numerous large upright fluted branches arising at or near the base, resembling organ pipes. The stems, to 8 inches thick with 12 to 19 low rounded ribs, carry numerous needle-like half-inch spines at the areoles.

The 3-inch nocturnal flowers may remain open the next day. At maturity the 3-inch fruits are olive-green, covered by dense deciduous spines.

41

**CEREUS SENILIS** (white-haired or old) Old-Man Cactus. Seedling Old-Man Cacti are favored by cactophiles, but their growth is so slow (between ¼ and 1 inch a year) that mature specimens are seldom seen. Where native in the states of Guanajuato and Hidalgo, Mexico, they cover the steep limestone slopes of the river valleys with their tall stately columns. Large plants, nearly 40 feet high must be several hundred years old.

The stems seldom branch above ground level, but branch freely from the base when old. The 20 to 30 ribs bear closely-set areoles filled with wavy white wool. When 18 feet high and first ready to flower, a pseudocephalium of spirally-arranged tubercles rather than ribs appears at the stem tip. From its areoles grow masses of dense tawny wool, short bristles, and the nocturnal flowers; fruit about 1 inch long.

**C. MACROSTIBAS** (literally, "big bed of straw" (Gr.), probably referring to the enlarged spiny areoles). This unusual species inhabits hillsides on the edges of the Peruvian Coastal Desert throughout western Peru under conditions of extremely low rainfall. Its moisture is largely provided by fog, dew, mist, or occasional winter drizzle. Its surroundings are rocky and barren. In this environment growth is slow.

These are stocky erect columnar cacti with many basal branches, 6 to 13 feet high. The foot-thick stems have 4 to 6 ribs separated by broad intervals. The unusual areoles, about an inch apart, enlarge to inch-wide spheres of brown felt, or, on old plants, may elongate to over 2 inches. Of the 12 or more spines at an areole, one or two lengthen up to 10 inches, and are the longest cactus spines known.

43

**CEREUS ALAMOSENSIS** (of Alamos, Sonora, where first discovered) Cina, ranges from Nayarit northward through Sinaloa to southern Sonora, Mexico.

Cinas are slender columns up to almost 10 feet high but only 3 inches thick, with from 5 to 8 bluntly-rounded ribs. Small areoles, spaced about an inch apart along the ribs, carry from 11 to 18 sharp spreading radial spines and 1 to 4 much stouter central spines with a length of 1 to 2 inches.

As the plants grow tall, the stem curves or bends over until it touches the ground; it then roots near the tip and forms new plants. This habit gives rise to large clusters of Cinas sometimes 25 feet in diameter.

The diurnal tubular flowers vary from 2 to 4 inches long, and open their petals obliquely at the throat. The globular red fruit measures 2½ inches.

**C. BAUMANNII** (for Charles and Constantine Baumann, French nurserymen) Firecracker Cactus; Scarlet Bugler, ranging from northern Argentina into Uruguay, Paraguay, and south-eastern Bolivia, has been known and cultivated for more than a century.

The thin columnar stems, only 1½ inches thick, reach a height of 6 feet; it sometimes has a few slender upright branches at the base, parallel to the main stem. The stems have 12 to 16 low broadly-rounded ribs divided by deep grooves. The closely spaced areoles bear clusters of 15 to 20 thin sharp spines up to an inch and a half long.

The diurnal flowers are zyg-omorphic, up to 3 inches long, with an S-shaped tube that ends in a slanting mouth. The petal tips do not open out-ward, but remain pointed for-ward. Blooms in summer.

**CEREUS LAMPROCHLORUS** (green torch), from northern Argentina, is similar in habit to the two preceding species, but is a more robust, stouter plant, often used as a rootstock for delicate young scions. Its upright cylindrical stems, 3 to 6½ feet tall, are 6 to 8 inches thick, at first unbranched, but later on branching from the base. New growth is bright green, contrasting sharply with the drab green older growth.

Stems have from 10 to 17 low ribs that are conspicuously wavy when young, becoming rounded and smoother with age. The areoles, about ½-inch apart, are armed with 11 to 14 short straight sharp-pointed radial spines, some strong and rigid, others bristle-like. The 4 central spines, to ¾-inch long, are somewhat stronger.

The showy nocturnal flowers, to 10 inches long and 6 inches wide, are borne freely.

**C. ERUCA** (to belch) Chirinola; Creeping Devil, crawls over the wind-drifted sand of the coastal plains of Baja California and Magdalena Island like monstrous caterpillars. The stems, 3 to 9 feet long and 3 inches thick, hug the sand except for their upraised heads.

The stems root along the lower side, slowly growing forward as the old stem gradually dies behind. When a stem meets an obstruction such as a log, rock, or fellow cactus, it raises its head, grows up one side and down the other, and by dying at the rear literally but slowly crosses the obstacle.

These cacti tend to grow in groups and are sand binders, preventing erosion and accumulating wind-blown sand. Desert foxes dig their burrows among the formidable spiny stems.

The attractive flowers, up to 5 inches long and 2 inches wide, are diurnal.

**CEREUS MARTIANUS** (for Karl F. P. von Martius, 1794-1868, Botany Professor at Munich and founder of the Flora Brasiliensis).

This cactus of central Mexico is a slender vine-like plant that creeps over the ground, climbs rocks and trees, and also grows as an epiphyte, hanging from the trunks and limbs of trees. The plant sends out aerial roots all along the stem, serve for anchorage and adsorption.

The stems are occasionally branched, about ¾-inch wide and several feet long, with 5 to 8 low rounded ribs. The areoles, about ½-inch apart, carry 6 to 10 short spines, needle-like to mere bristles.

The tubular diurnal flowers, 3 to 4 inches long, are produced profusely. Individual flowers open early in the morning and remain open several days. The spiny fruits are ¾-inch globular berries.

**C. FLAGELLIFORMIS** (whip-like) Rat-Tail Cactus, is similar in growth habit to the preceding species, but is better known. It has been cultivated throughout Mexico, Central, and South America for its flowers, apparently since pre-Columbian times, and is not known in the wild state. It probably originated in Mexico.

Young plants hold their stems upward, but they are weak and become prostrate as they elongate. The 10 to 12 low ribs are slightly tubercled; the areoles, ¼-inch apart, bear 8 to 12 radial and 3 or 4 central spines.

The 3-inch diurnal flowers appear in February and March; individual flowers stay open for 3 or 4 days. The ½-inch round red bristle-covered fruits have yellow pulp.

Hybrids with other Cereus have produced many forms in a variety of hues.

**CEREUS EMORYI** (for Lieut.-Col. William H. Emory, 1811-1887, in charge of the Mexican Boundary Survey) Velvet Cactus, grows at elevations of 200 feet or less on sandy dry hills and bluffs near the coast from Del Mar, San Diego County, California, southward into northwestern Baja California. It is common on Santa Catalina and San Clemente Islands.

This cactus is a shrub with sprawling branches covered by dense clear yellow spines that hide the joints; in age the spines blacken. It multiplies by sending out branches from beneath the sand, forming colonies several yards in diameter. The cylindrical joints are 1 to 2 feet long and 1½ to 2 inches thick, with 12 to 16 inconspicuous ribs. Spines are clustered 20 to 30 per areole; the 2-inch chief one bent backward, the others pointing in all directions. It flowers in May.

50

**C. SPEGAZZINII** (for Carlos Spegazzini, 1858-1926, Argentine botanist) is native to the sub-tropical seasonally-arid Chacos of northeastern Argentina and Paraguay. The plants are erect when young, but the stems and branches begin to bend or curve as they reach several feet in length. The stems are about an inch wide, strongly 3-angled, with toothed margins; the tips of the teeth bear the areoles.

Spines on young branches are brown or black, only 3 to an areole, but 3 more develop in the areoles on the older parts of the stems.

The gray-green flower buds and the open flowers are held rigidly erect, but after closing they turn and point downward.

As a pot-plant, it is prized for its marbled stems. Free-blooming, it bears two or more crops of 4- to 5-inch nocturnal flowers in early summer.

51

**CEREUS CAVENDISHII** (for William G. S. Cavendish, 1790-1858, 6th Duke of Devonshire) ranges from northern Argentina and Paraguay into Brazil (Sao Paulo); its northern limits are uncertain.

The long slender cylindrical stems, up to 10 feet long and about an inch wide, mostly branch from near the base and sprawl to form an open spreading shrub, or clamber over the surrounding vegetation to form thickets. The 9 or 10 ribs are low and rounded, with small areoles about ⅓-inch apart and set with 8 to 12 needle-like radial spines and 1 to 3 central spines to ¾-inch long.

This species is considered to be the most prolific bloomer of all cacti. The tubular flowers, 4 to 5 inches long, open at night and appear abundantly from April to September.

The 2-inch plump round red fruits are spineless.

**C. SERPENTINUS**, Snake or Serpent Cactus, is a common Mexican garden flower. Although found half-wild in hedges or running over abandoned walls, it is not known as a wild plant.

At first a columnar upright clump of stems 3 feet high, but later on hanging or creeping as it elongates to 10 feet. Underground, it forms a cluster of large turnip-like tubers at the base of the stems; these are water and food-storage organs.

The sinuous stems, 1 to 2 inches thick, have 10 to 13 low rounded ribs. The closely-set felted areoles bear about 12 spines to 1 inch long, varying from needle-like to bristles.

A profusion of 6-inch nocturnal flowers appear in May and June, and emit the most delicious perfume of all cacti. Fruits set freely; they ripen to 1½-inch red ovals covered by deciduous spines. The pulp is red, seeds few but large.

53

**CEREUS POSELGERI** (for Heinrich Poselger, died 1883, German cactologist) Sacasil, inhabits semi-desert scrub and brushlands of southern Texas near the Rio Grande, and of the states of Tamaulipas, Nuevo Leon, and Coahuila in northeastern Mexico.

From a cluster of tuberous roots near the surface of the soil it sends up thin round stems a little thicker than a lead pencil and up to 2 feet long. The stems and branches are thin and spineless at the base, thicker towards the tip and hidden by the spines flattened against it. A common plant but hard to find, as it grows under scrub and rests its stems in the lower branches.

The diurnal 1½-inch flowers appear from February to April. They open about noon and close at night, each one opening and closing in this way for several days.

**C. GREGGII** (for Dr. J. Gregg, student of cacti and plant explorer of northern Mexico) Desert Night-Blooming Cereus, grows among bushes and shrubs along flats and washes in the deserts of northern Mexico from Sonora to Tamaulipas, and across southern Arizona, New Mexico, and Texas to the Pecos River.

The slender dark brittle stems arise from a huge turnip-shaped tuber that can weigh over 40 pounds. The Mexicans and native Indians know it as "Saramatraca," and use it for medicinal purposes.

Flowering occurs late in May or in June, and most of the flowers open on just one or two nights of the year. They begin opening an hour before sundown, closing soon after sunrise. A single bloom scents the air for a hundred feet around with a spicy arbutus-like perfume. The red fruit is delicious.

**CEREUS BONPLANDII** (for Amié J. A. Bonpland, 1773-1858, French naturalist and explorer) Midnight Lady, grows among trees and shrubs in the Chacos of northern Argentina and Paraguay, and ranges into southern Brazil. Its grayish-green stems, to 10 feet long and only 1 to 2 inches thick, are strongly 4-angled.

Plants are branched from the base and first erect, then arching and sprawling or clamber-ing, or if without support finally prostrate and creeping. The areoles, ¾-inch apart, are armed with 6 to 8 needle-like spines up to 1½ inches long.

The flowers, 6 to 9 inches long and as wide, open after dark and close soon after sun-rise. The main flowering period is May and June, but under favorable conditions it flowers freely all year. The spineless but scaly red globular fruits, about 2 inches long, are edible.

**CEREUS LEMAIREI** (for Charles Lemaire, 1800-1871, Belgian botanist) Night-Blooming Cereus, a very beautiful species from Trinidad and Tobago, has long been known in cultivation. In its native habitat it grows as a slender high-climbing vine, scaling the tree trunks by means of copious aerial roots.

The inch-wide stems are 3-angled, but the ribs are thickened at their base so that the stem is virtually triangular in cross-section. The areoles, about an inch apart, usually have 2 very short spines with bulbous bases. The rib margins are slightly raised under the areoles, producing a somewhat notched or toothed aspect.

The nocturnal flowers, almost a foot long, are unusual in having forked stigma-lobes. Fortunately, the blooms are not strongly scented, as their odor is unpleasant. Fruits are oblong, purple when ripe.

57

**CEREUS SPECIOSUS** (showy) Xoalacatl; Santa Marta; Sun Cereus, native to central Mexico, is common on stony soils and outcrops in the Valley of Mexico, and on the rocky slopes of the surrounding mountains.

These plants branch freely at the base, forming large masses of succulent stems that climb over the rocks, holding on by sending out roots here and there along their length.

The inch-thick branches are strongly angled, with 3 to 5 wavy ribs; the older parts are bright green, contrasting with the reddish tips. Areoles are often over an inch apart, with many short needle-like spines.

Diurnal flowers appear throughout spring and each one lasts several days. This flower, known to horticulturists since 1803, has been much hybridized with species of Epiphyllum and other cacti.

**C. OCAMPONIS** (of Ocampo, probably referring to the town in SW Tamaulipas, Mexico) is not known as a wild plant. Some European botanists describe it as native to Colombia, but Colombian botanists are sure it originated elsewhere. This and a few other Cereus, described as distinct species, resemble C. *undatus* (p. 60).

Cereus ocamponis has strongly 3-angled elongated clambering stems and branches that run over rocks and walls. Young stems are bright green with deep wavy ribs, the areoles at the bottom of each wave; old stems turn dull bluish-green, and the rib margins become brown and horny.

The nocturnal flowers are a foot long and equally broad. The oval fruit, over 4 inches wide, is covered by broad overlapping red scales with pointed tips. The wine-red pulp is bland and sweet.

59

**CEREUS UNDATUS** (wavy, referring to the rib margins) Queen of the Night, carried round the world by the Spanish and Portuguese in the 16th Century, is widely cultivated and now half-wild in all tropical countries. Truly wild plants are in the mountain forests of Martinique, and two wild forms common to Yucatan.

This cactus is a long-stemmed high-climbing vine, often 20 to 40 feet long, with aerial roots.

The stems are mostly 3-angled, the thin inch-wide ribs have wavy margins that become horny in age. Huge nocturnal flowers appear in summer.

This plant forms the celebrated half-mile hedge around Punshou College, Honolulu, planted in the 1830's by Sibyl M. Bingham, which produces as many as 5000 flowers a night during flowering season.

The rosy fruits have delicious crisp white pulp.

60

**C. MARTINII,** a much-branched clambering Argentine species, is very free-flowering and easy to cultivate.

Young stems are vigorous, less than an inch thick, 4- or 5-angled, in age elongating to 6 feet or more and becoming nearly cylindrical. The areoles bear a few short radial spines and 1 stout central spine about an inch long; old branches are nearly spineless.

The flowers are nocturnal, about 8 inches long, with scales on both the flower-tube and ovary carrying tufts of brown felt in their axils. Flower coloration differs between individual plants; in some, the broad inner petals are pure white, in others suffused with pink as illustrated.

The brilliant carmine fruits, 1½ inches wide, retain the small scales that were on the ovary, and the withered flower remains attached to its apex.

61

**CEREUS ERIOPHORUS** (wool bearing) Jíjira, grows in forests and thickets throughout Cuba and the Isle of Pines, and occasionally on rather open hillsides as well.

The plants are usually less than 3 feet high, bushy, with bright green erect or upraised cylindrical stems and branches 1½ inches thick. The 8 or 9 ribs are prominent, with rather deep grooves between them. The areoles are about an inch apart, each with 6 to 9 sharp spines up to 1½ inches long.

Young flower buds are swathed in long bright white wool which grows in the axils of the scales on the flower-tube; it is mostly shed as the buds reach full size and open. The funnel-formed flowers, 5 to 10 inches long, are nocturnal. The bright yellow globose fruits, over 2 inches wide, have small tufts of short white hairs scattered over the skin.

**C. ERIOPHORUS** var. **FRAGRANS** (fragrant) has a limited natural range and is in danger of extinction. It inhabits Atlantic coastal hammocks of high sanddunes, kitchen middens, and coquina ledges in mid-peninsular Florida, from Mosquito Inlet to St. Lucie Sound. Much of this ocean front is rapidly being developed and "improved" by cutting these jungle hammocks, and this cactus is becoming harder to find.

This variety differs from the species proper in that the stems reach a length of 15 feet, are first upright, then reclining or conspicuously clambering as they elongate. The 10 to 12 ribs bear areoles containing 9 to 13 sharp needle-like spines.

The flowers are nocturnal, bell-shaped when open, 6 to 8 inches long, and fragrant; the inner petals vary from white to pink. The mature fruits are dull orange in color.

63

**CEREUS STENOPTERUS** (narrow-winged, referring to the ribs) grows as a weak vine in the forests of Costa Rica; its light green 3-angled stems are easily overlooked unless the plant is in flower.

The stems, 1½ inches wide, produce aerial roots sparingly, and the plant is not a vigorous climber. Areoles are slightly raised along the edge of the 3 thin ribs, and armed with 1 to 3 small yellow spines.

The nocturnal flowers, about 4 inches long and 6 wide, open well after dark and close early the next morning; they are generally completely closed by 9 am. These flowers are distinctive in several ways: the flower-tube above the ovary is short, only ¾-inch in length; the perianth-segments are all similarly linear in form, and all the same color. This species is easy to grow as a pot plant, and flowers frequently.

**C. URBANIANUS** (for Ignatius Urban, 1848-1931, German botanist) is a climbing or clambering vine of Cuba and Hispaniola with aerial roots, often reaching into the treetops, or trailing over rocks or shrubs when growing in the open.

The stems and branches, over an inch thick, are much elongated and succulent, usually with 4 or 5 ribs, but sometimes with 3 or 6. The light green stems occasionally become a deep reddish-purple throughout the entire plant. The small white-felted areoles bear clusters of short spines at the upper side, and longer white bristles or hairs which point backward from the lower side.

The nocturnal flowers, up to 12 inches long, have nearly a hundred thin orange-brown perianth segments surrounding the white inner petals. Areoles on the flower-tube and ovary bear long white tufts of hair.

**CEREUS TONDUZII** (for A. Tonduz, Costa Rican naturalist, who discovered it in 1898) Flor de Bailarina (Ballerina-Flower) is a climbing tree-dwelling cactus from the high mountain slopes on the Pacific side of Costa Rica, living in rather dry woodland just below the cloud forests.

The plant is a branching epiphyte, the joints 4 to 16 or more inches long, cylindrical at the base, mostly 3-angled above, about an inch thick. Areoles are slightly raised, producing faint notches on the margins. Young areoles have 1 to 6 short bristle-like spines, easily detached and soon lost; old stems are spineless. Aerial roots abound.

Flowers in spring, so freely that the buds hide the stem; the 3-inch funnelform flowers have dark sharp spines and tufts of black wool in areoles on the flower-tube and ovary.

**C. TUNILLA** (for the vernacular Spanish name, meaning "little cactus fruit") Tunilla, a fast-growing tropical epiphytic vine from the jungles of Panama and Costa Rica, is seldom seen in cultivation. It climbs by means of aerial roots; stems and branches hang from the trunks and limbs of trees.

Young plants have nearly cylindrical stems; in adults the stems are usually strongly 4-angled, rarely from 2- to 5-angled. The felted areoles carry tufts of 6 to 12 short stiff spines with bulbous bases, spreading in all directions.

This species flowers profusely; the rosy nocturnal flowers, about 3 inches long, are borne singly at the areoles and emit a pleasing fragrance. The oval tuberculate fruits, 1¾ inches long and 1½ wide, have a smooth shiny light pink skin and a few areoles bearing wool and about 6 bristles.

67

**CEREUS SETACEUS** (bristly) Cardó Ananaz (Pineapple Cactus) Braz., is a strong climber ranging from central Brazil into Argentina, much cultivated in South America and sometimes half-wild in other countries.

The elongate stems and branches, 1-3 inches thick, are 3-5 angled, but 3 is the usual condition. Areoles first bear 10-15 white deciduous bristles, followed by a few short conical spines with swollen bases.

The foot-long nocturnal flowers are followed by large yellow tuberculate fruits, about 4 inches long and 3 wide. The areoles at the tips of the tubercles bear deciduous spines over half an inch long. The exquisite flavor of the pulp makes them so sought for by monkeys that it is hard to find a ripe fruit on wild plants. This species is cultivated for its fruits, which bring a good price in South American markets.

**C. WITTII** (for Mr. N. H. Witt of Manaus, Brazil, who collected it for botanical study) grows around tree-trunks in the Varzea forests of Amazonas and Pará, Brazil; these forests also surround the *Igapó* (permanent swampland). Trees of Varzea forests are distinct from upland jungle species.

This cactus has jointed leaf-like flattened stems, rarely with 3 angles. The joints, to 16 inches long and 4 wide, cling by aerial roots from the under side of the midrib. Areoles, about ½-inch apart, have compact tufts of white wool and 20 or more thin brittle prickly spines from ½ to 2 inches long.

The 9-inch nocturnal flowers appear at lateral areoles. The small oval fruit is tubercled, with woolly hairs and slender yellow spines at the areoles.

This species is a "link" between Cereus and genus Epiphyllum (see the next page).

69

**EPIPHYLLUM,** with about 20 species, ranges from Mexico through Central America into tropical South America. These Cacti are upright flat-stemmed much-branched plants of epiphytic habit, growing on trees but not parasitic, obtaining the moisture necessary for their development from the air.

The main stem is often a thin woody cylinder, but the branches are usually much flattened and leaf-like, with scalloped or toothed margins and small areoles in the notches along the margin. True leaves are lacking. Mature plants lack spines, which are represented in seedlings and juvenile forms by slender bristles.

Flowers arise from the marginal areoles; the tube is always longer than the diameter of the open flower, in some greatly elongated. Flowers in some species nocturnal, in others diurnal, either odorless or very fragrant, usually showy, similar to those of some species of Cereus. The fruit is edible.

**E. OXYPETALUM** (sharp-petaled) is "Night-Blooming Cereus" to innumerable Americans who grow it as a house plant. In maturity a stout plant over 6 feet tall, with numerous leaf-like side branches carried in the same plane as the main stem. Huge flowers appear from May to November.

**E. PHYLLANTHUS** (leaf-flowering, referring to flowers from leaf-like branches) var. *pittieri* (for Henri Pittier, botanist, 1857-1950) is common in jungle on the Atlantic side of Costa Rica below 3000 feet. It forms densely-branched masses on trees. The 3½-inch flowers are the smallest in the genus.

**E. DARRAHII** (for Charles Darrah, English cactus fancier, 1844-1903) blooms freely during late summer and early fall. Individual flowers open at evening and remain open from 40 to 48 hours, emitting a delicious honeysuckle fragrance. The fruits, green in color, are tart and agreeable.

**E. ACKERMANNII** (for George Ackermann, who discovered it in Mexico in 1828) has been grown ever since, but wild plants were recently rediscovered in Vera Cruz and Oaxaca, between 6000 and 8000 feet above sea level. Flowers are diurnal. Forma *candida*, of Chiapas, is white-flowered.

**EPIPHYLLUM HYBRIDS**, prized for the spectacular variety of form and color of their flowers, were first developed by European breeders in the 19th Century. Early crosses with species of Cereus produced a race of day-blooming large-flowered cacti, easy to grow, sometimes called "orchid cacti." Strong-

growing plants, they require more room than the average house plant. Later crosses with species of Rhipsalis (pp. 74-76) and Nopalxochia (p. 77) gave a race of compact habit, perfect for indoors. Today over 3000 registered hybrids are cultivated; flowers vary from ¼ inch to a foot in diameter.

**RHIPSALIS,** broadly interpreted, contains about 70 mostly epiphytic species of diverse form. The stems are jointed and much-branched; joints may be either slender and thread-like, or stout and stiff. They may be cylindrical, angled, or much flattened and leaf-like. Areoles are tiny, borne along the margins of flat-jointed species, but along the midribs or scattered irregularly in others, and carry hairs, wool, bristles, spines, or a part of these.

The flowers, small in comparison with those of other cacti, have relatively few petals and usually lack a tube. In most species they open only once, day or night, and remain open from 1 to 8 days. The fruit is usually a juicy globular berry with sticky seeds.

Ranging from Florida, Mexico, and the West Indies through continental America to Argentina, a few are also found in Africa and Ceylon, probably because seed stuck to the feet of birds of passage.

**R. HOULETTIANA** (for Houlett, a French gardener) Snowdrop Cactus, is epiphytic on trees in the mountains of south-central Brazil at elevations of 3000 feet. The plant, resembling an Epiphyllum, has stems over 6 feet long, cylindrical below but flattened above, with leaf-like branches.

**R. WARMINGIANA** (for Johannes Warming, Danish botanist, 1841-1924) Popcorn Cactus, from Minas Gerais, Brazil, is erect when young, spreading or hanging with age. The elongated jointed branches are either flat or sharply 3- or 4-angled. Hyacinth-scented flowers; fruits are purple.

**R. PACHYPTERA** (thick-winged) has erect or pendant much-branched stems to 3 feet long, composed of broad thick joints which are usually flat but occasionally 3-angled. The joints, 2 to 8 inches long and up to 5 inches broad, become tinged with purple if grown in strong light. It is also Brazilian.

**R. PARADOXA** (unusual) Chain or Link Cactus, hangs in large clusters of sparingly-branched stems 3 feet long, made up of short 3-winged joints that are twisted as they link together, so that the angles of one joint alternate with a flat side of the next. Brazilian, with the flowers ¾ of an inch wide.

**RHIPSALIS GRANDIFLORA** (large-flowered), from the state of Rio de Janeiro, Brazil, has stout tubular jointed stems to 3 feet long and over ⅜ of an inch in diameter. Its branches are held widely apart; the ultimate short branchlets are whorled at the stem tip.

The faintly-scented wheel-shaped flowers arise in mid-winter from areoles scattered all along the joints; they are nearly 1 inch wide.

**R. CEREUSCULA** (like a little wax candle) Rice Cactus, forms erect clumps 2 feet high on forest trees from Uruguay to central Brazil. The thin round stems and branches are crowned by clusters of short angled twigs which carry tiny bristles in the areoles.

Unlike most Rhipsalis, this species produces flowers at or near the branch tips. The fruits are white berries which resemble those of mistletoe.

**NOPALXOCHIA**, a genus of dubious validity, contains one or two species formerly classified as Epiphyllum. When fully open, the flowers are as wide or wider than the flower tube is long. *E. ackermannii* (p. 70) is sometimes put into Nopalxochia.

**N. PHYLLANTHOIDES** (Phyllanthuslike) Deutsche Kaiserin (German Empress) has a discontinuous natural range: it is found in the state of Puebla, Mexico, at 5000 feet elevation, and also in the Magdalena Valley, Colombia, where it is called "Rabo de Iguana" (Lizard's-Tail). One of the oldest of cultivated cacti, first described by Hernández in 1651.

77

**SCHLUMBERGERA** contains a few epiphytic Brazilian cacti with branched stems made up of short mostly flattened joints with scalloped or toothed margins. Allied to both Epiphyllum and Zygocactus, the terminal sharp-petaled flowers and the fruits are distinctive. The fruits are held by the plant long after maturing.

**S. GAERTNERI** (for Gaertner, who discovered it circa 1882 near Blumenau, Sao Paulo, Brazil) Easter Cactus, is an upright tree-dwelling plant with hanging branch-tips. Terminal joints often have bristles at the tip. The flowers, to 3 inches broad, are produced in profusion during March and April.

**ZYGOCACTUS** is a monotypic genus from the Organ Mountains, Rio de Janeiro, Brazil, epiphytic on trees. Similar in habit to Schlumbergera, the stems branch by forking, and are composed of numerous short flat joints that become rounded in age. Flowers are terminal, tubular, and conspicuously zygomorphic.

**Z. TRUNCATUS** (cut off square, referring to the joint tips) Crab Cactus, long grown for its late fall flowers, has been so much hybridized with species of Epiphyllum, Schlumbergera, and Cereus that typical plants are rarely seen. Over 200 varieties are cultivated; fruits only if cross-pollinated.

**ECHINOCEREUS** (Hedgehog Cacti) contains between 20 and 30 species, some with many botanical varieties. The species range from near Mexico City north to California, South Dakota, and Oklahoma.

The stems of some are solitary, of others branching and clump-forming, sometimes of 500 stems. The larger stems are cylindric, 2 to 24 inches long, 1 to 4 inches thick, with 5 to 12 ribs composed of tubercles that coalesce from half to nearly all their height. The spines are smooth; central spines are flattened or needle-like, the radials always needle-like.

Flowers are borne on old growth and are located below the stem apex. The flower buds push through the epidermis just above the spiny areole and are not attached to it; flowers leave a persistent scar on the stem. The flowers are from ¾ to 5 inches across.

The fruits are fleshy when ripe, globular or oval, from ¼ to 2 inches long, ¼ to 1½ inches wide; their skin has deciduous spine-bearing areoles.

**E. TRIGLOCHIDIATUS** (with 3 barbed bristles) Claret-Cup, shows how a single species can vary. The typical form ranges from NE Arizona and S Colorado to W-central and central New Mexico, has few stems, 5 to 8 tuberculate ribs, and 3-angled spines.

**VAR. MOJAVENSIS,** Mojave Hedgehog forms clumps up to 500 stems, usually has 9 or 10 tuberculate ribs, and twisted central spines. It grows in S Nevada, SE California, NW Arizona, and SW Utah at elevations of 3500 to 8000 or even 10,000 feet.

**VAR. MELANACANTHUS** (with black spines) Red Hedgehog, also forms clumps of 500 stems, mostly with 9-10 tuberculate ribs, and deflexed central spines. It ranges from upland Arizona, central Utah, S Colorado and SW Texas to Durango, Mexico.

**VAR. NEOMEXICANUS,** New Mexican Claret-Cup, makes small clumps of 5 to 45 stems, has 8-12 but usually 10 ribs, the tubercles obscure, its central spines needle-like. It grows from NW Mexico across Trans-Pecos, Texas to S New Mexico and SE Arizona.

**ECHINOCEREUS BLANCKII** (for P. A. Blanck, a Berlin pharmacist) Devil's Finger, shade-loving, grows at low elevations in fine soils inside thickets in NE Mexico and S Texas.

The plants have many stems, the joints mostly 2-6 inches long with 5-6 ribs, which are prominent and strongly tuberculate on new growth, indistinct on older parts. Flowers open about noon and close about 5 pm for 3 consecutive days. It seldom sets fruit.

**E. BLANCKII** var. **ANGUSTICEPS** (narrow-headed) Yellow Alicoche is a sun-loving variety restricted to light sandy limestone loams and desert conditions at low elevations in S Texas, from Bexar County southward; difficult to cultivate.

This variety forms small clumps of 1 to 10 stems; the joints, from 4-7 inches long and to 1¼ inches wide, are soft, weak, and sprawling, with 7-9 strongly tuberculate ribs. The flowers are fragrant.

**E. PENTALOPHUS** (five-crested) Alicoche grows in fine soils from NE Mexico into S Texas.

The stems branch to form clumps; the joints, to 4 inches long and 1 inch thick, have 4 or 5 low ribs and resemble 4 or 5-sided prisms. Joints root at the areoles, and old clumps are 10 to 15 feet across.

The flowers, 3 to 4 inches wide, appear in May or June. The oval fruit, to ½-inch long, is green with brown spines and masses of white wool.

**E. VIRIDIFLORUS** (green-flowered) Green Pitaya, ranges from South Dakota to E Wyoming, E Colorado, Oklahoma, New Mexico, and the Texas Panhandle; its varieties range to the Big Bend, Texas.

The stems are solitary or in clumps of 6 or less, cylindrical, to 3 inches tall and to 1½ inches wide, with 10 to 14 ribs.

The inch-wide flowers appear in April or May. The oval fruit is a half-inch long, with white wool and white spines.

83

**ECHINOCEREUS PECTINATUS** (comb-like) Comb Hedgehog. Typical plants inhabit limestone hills and flats, both in grassland and desert, from San Luis Potosi, Mexico, to SE Arizona, and along the Rio Grande, Texas, east to Maverick County.

The stems, solitary or with 2 or 3 branches, are 4-12 inches tall, up to 4 thick. It has 3-5 central spines set in 1 or sometimes 2 vertical rows, and 12-16 radials per areole.

**E. PECTINATUS var. WENIGERI** (for Del Weniger, American biologist) Comb Hedgehog is found in northern Coahuila, Mexico, and in Texas on the Edwards Plateau in Terrell, Val Verde, and Sutton Counties.

Its stems are similar to those of the typical form, but the 1 to 3 ashy-white central spines are always set in 1 vertical row, and the 14 to 16 radials often curve back so that their tips are down between the ribs.

84

**E. PECTINATUS** var. **NEOMEXI-CANUS** (of New Mexico) Texas Rainbow Cactus, ranges from Chihuahua, Mexico, into SE Arizona, and from SE New Mexico to Culberson and Brewster Counties, Texas.

Old plants may develop 5 or 6 stems, 3 or 7 to 9 central spines in 2 or 3 vertical rows, and 18-22 radials per areole; these and the yellow flowers make this variety distinct from the others.

**E. PECTINATUS** var. **RIGIDISSI-MUS** (very stiff spines) Arizona Rainbow Cactus grows from northern Chihuahua and Sonora, Mexico, to S Arizona and SW New Mexico.

The areoles have no central spines; the 18-22 radials are in an orderly array, in alternating band of red and white.

As is true of most Hedgehog Cacti, the stigma-lobes remain closed until the pollen is no longer viable in that flower.

**ECHINOCEREUS LLOYDII** (for F. E. Lloyd, 1868-1947, Canadian botanist, who discovered it), from SE New Mexico and Pecos County, Texas, grows in gravelly or sandy soils at about 3000 feet elevation.

The plants are at first solitary, becoming large before branching to form clumps of 5 or 6 stems, which are cylindric, to 8 inches high and 4 thick. The 12 ribs have round areoles bearing 2-5 central spines and 8-9 radials.

**E. SCHEERI** (for Frederick Scheer 1792-1868, German botanist) from central Chihuahua, Mexico, has long flowertube, to almost 5 inches.

The plants branch freely from the base, forming dense clumps. The stems either lie flat, curve upward, or are erect. They are about 8 inches long and an inch thick, slightly tapered toward the tip, with 8-10 low ribs. The areoles have 3 red central spines and 7-9 white-tipped radials.

**E. CHLORANTHUS** (green-flow-ered) grows in limestone at elevations of 3000 to 4500 feet, ranging from northern Mexico to SE New Mexico and to Texas west of the Pecos River.

The stems, solitary or rarely with 1 or 2 branches, are 3-7 inches high, 2½-3 thick, with 10 to 14 ribs. Areoles have 5-6 central spines; the 15-20 radial spines, set in 2 rows, are so dense they hide the stem. The inch-wide flowers are green to bronze or red-brown.

**E. ROETTERI** (for Paulus Roetter, artist, who drew the cacti of the Mexican Boundary Survey) is today a rare species, known only from SE New Mexico.

The stems are solitary, to 6 inches tall and 3 inches thick, with 10-13 tuberculate ribs. The areoles are armed with 2-5 stout central spines and 8-15 radials, some of which are very tiny and bristle-like; all the spines have bulbous bases.

The brilliant purple flowers are 2 to 3 inches long.

**ECHINOCEREUS REICHENBACHII** (for H. L. G. Reichenbach, 1793-1879, German botanist and zoologist) Lace Cactus, common on limestone or gypsum hills, is shown with 3 of its varieties. Typical forms range from central Texas north over most of Oklahoma.

Stems are solitary or in clumps, usually 3-5 inches tall (rarely to 16), 1-2 inches wide, with 12-18 ribs. The areoles lack central spines; radials curve in a low arc.

**VAR. ALBISPINUS** (white-spined), of the Oklahoma and Texas Panhandles, often branches freely to form dense clumps of stems, often smaller than the typical form, 3-6 inches tall and 1 inch thick.

The areoles have 1-3 central spines; the 12-14 straight radial spines, not comb-like in arrangement, are spread out all around the areole. The spine tips vary in color between individual plants, and may be white, red, yellow, or brown.

**VAR. PERBELLUS** (very beautiful) is found in SE Colorado, E New Mexico, and NW Texas.

The stems, either solitary or in branching clusters, are usually not over 4 inches high, with 13-15 low broad ribs. Central spines 0-1, so tiny as to be easily overlooked. The 12 to 16 or 20 straight radial spines spread a little irregularly; they vary from pink to straw-color. This variety, a favorite of collectors, flowers freely from March to June.

**VAR. PURPUREUS** (purple) Black Lace Cactus, from the Wichita and Glass Mountains of western Oklahoma, is hard to find in the wild, and seldom seen in cactus collections.

The stems and growth habit are similar to typical plants. There are 0-3 central spines and 14-22 radials per areole, curved and comb-like, but the outer part of each spine is a dark purple to nearly jet black. The purple flowers are either green- or red-throated.

**ECHINOCEREUS ENGELMANNII** (for George Engelmann, 1809-1884, cactologist, Missouri Botanical Garden) var. *acicularis* (needle-like) Strawberry Hedgehog grows mostly in the Arizona Desert; other varieties range from N Baja California and N Sonora to S California and Utah.

The stems, usually 5-15 in a clump, are 6-8 inches long, to 2 thick. Fruits are highly prized by the Pima Indians.

**E. FENDLERI** (for August Fendler, 1813-1883, botanical collector) var. *rectispinus* (straight-spined) Purple Hedgehog, lives in grassland, from 3900 to 6800 feet, in SE Arizona, SW New Mexico, and from El Paso to Culberson Co., Texas.

Stems are single (rarely to 5), 4-10 inches tall, about 2 thick, with 8-10 ribs. All spines are straight; the 1 central per areole is held straight out at a right angle to the stem.

**E. BAILEYI** (for Vernon Bailey, 1864-1942, chief field naturalist, U. S. Geological Survey) is restricted to granitic mountainsides of SW Oklahoma, but is common in the Wichita Mountains Wildlife Refuge.

Rarely solitary, forming dense clumps of 20-30 stems, to 8 inches tall and 3½ thick; stems have 15 ribs. Areoles have 0-5 central spines and 12-28 radials that interlock with those from the adjacent areoles.

**E. LEDINGII** (for A. R. Leding, cactus enthusiast) prefers sandy or gravelly mountain slopes at 4000 to 6000 feet elevation. It grows in grassland, woodland, and chaparral in SE Arizona.

This cactus forms clumps of 4 to 10 stems 10-20 inches long and up to 3 inches thick, with 12-16 ribs. Areoles have 1-4 central spines curved at the base to point downward, plus 9-11 radials; spines are yellow, but blacken in age.

91

**ECHINOCEREUS ENNEACANTH-US** (nine-spined) Warty Hedgehog, grows on well-drained gravelly slopes; in Texas mostly in the lower Rio Grande Valley within 50 miles of the river and E of the Pecos; in Mexico in Chihuahua, Coahuila, and Nuevo Leon States.

Clump-forming, with stems to 12 inches long and 2 thick, mostly with 8-10 ribs; 7-12 spines per areole. The fragrant fruits are delicious.

**E. ENNEACANTHUS** var. **STRAMINEUS** (straw-colored) Spine-Mound; Strawberry Cactus, lives on very dry sandy or rocky hillsides in N Chihuahua, S New Mexico, and west of the Pecos in Texas.

This variety forms mounds of 350 or more stems, hidden under a mass of spines.

Plants flower in spring and set much fruit; when ripe their aroma and flavor are like strawberry preserves.

**E. ENNEACANTHUS** var. **DU-BIUS** (dubious), with much the same range as var. *stramineus*, prefers the sandy fans at the base of the hills, nearer the valley floor. It forms loose clumps of flabby reclining stems not hidden by the spines.

The tapering stems, to 15 or more inches long and 2-4 thick, have broad rounded ribs. The plants flower and fruit sparingly; the fruits, covered by deciduous spines, are edible.

**E. DELAETII** (for Frantz de Laet, Belgian cactus dealer) Old Lady, from the foothills of the Sierra Madre Oriental in SW Coahuila, Mexico, resembles a young *Cereus senilis* (p. 42), its stems hidden by long white curling hair-like bristles.

Clump-forming, the stems are seldom over 8 inches tall, with 17-20 ribs; there are 4-5 long red bristle-like central spines per areole. The flowers open in the forenoon and close at night.

**ECHINOPSIS** (Hedgehog or Easter Lily Cacti), with about 45 true species and many forms and hybrids, is native to southern South America east of the Andes. Stems are solitary or branched at the base to form clumps, globular to cylindric in form, seldom more than a foot high, with 9 to 24 sharp-angled ribs. Areoles are circular, distinct, borne on the ribs, woolly or felted, armed with 0 to 6 central spines and 3 to 16 radials. All spines are smooth and needle-like.

Flower buds arise just above the spine clusters in old areoles on growth of previous seasons, but may appear from near the stem apex to well down towards the base. The flowers are usually long and trumpet-shaped, opening at dusk or a little later and remaining open for 1, 2, or 3 days if satisfactory weather prevails. The flower-tube is scaly; the scales carry long hairs and a few rigid bristles in their axils. The fruit splits open on one side when ripe.

**E. MULTIPLEX** (many-folded, referring to the deep ribs) Pink Easter Lily Cactus, of southern Brazil, withstands winters out-of-doors in the milder parts of Canada. Plants may form large clumps; a clump in a Los Angeles garden bore 42 flower buds at once. Flowers first appear in spring.

**E. OBREPANDA** (turned upward, referring to the recurved spines) Violet Easter Lily Cactus, of Bolivia, has a globose or somewhat flattened stem with 17-18 thin prominent ribs. The one central spine is curved upward. The flowers, 8 inches long, have an abundance of black wool on the tube.

**E. SILVESTRII** (for Argentine zoologist Philip Silvestri) White Easter Lily Cactus, from the mountains of NW Argentina, is a compact-growing species 2-4 inches tall with 12-14 ribs, forming small clumps. Flowers are large, 6-8 inches long and 4 inches wide, produced freely, scentless day and night.

**E. TUBIFLORA** (trumpet-flowered) Bronze Easter Lily Cactus, from S Brazil and NW Argentina, has globular flattened stems about 5 inches wide, usually with 12 slightly undulate ribs. The stems branch from the base, forming small clumps. The flowers, 6-8 inches long, arise at the side of the stem.

**ECHINOPSIS LEUCANTHA** (white-flowered, something of a misnomer) Rose Easter Lily Cactus is native to western Argentina. Young stems become cylindric and about 14 inches tall in age, with 12-14 compressed ribs. The closely-set areoles carry 1 curved central spine and 8 much shorter radials.

Flowers open in the afternoon; closing the next morning about 10 o'clock.

**E. CALOCHLORA** (beautiful green) Shining Ball Cactus; Chartreuse Easter Lily Cactus, from Goias, Brazil, is a tropical frost-sensitive species. The plants are small spheres 2-4 inches in diameter, with 13 wide ribs. The areoles are armed with 3-4 central and 10-14 radial spines, all similar, yellow, and needle-like. The tube of the flowers is covered by fawn-colored hair.

**E. OXYGONA** (sharp-angled, referring to the perianth-segments) Red Easter Lily Cactus, ranging from S Brazil across Uruguay to NE Argentina, is also a cold-tolerant species. Stems are large flattened globes 10 inches across, with 14 ribs. The spines are clustered about 14 per areole. The flowers are sometimes nearly a foot long, with a very slender tube and pale red petals.

**E. AUREA** (golden) Golden Easter Lily Cactus, from NW Argentina, has stems only 2-4 inches wide, with 14-15 sharp-edged ribs separated by deep intervals; it is far smaller in proportion to *E. oxygona* than the painting indicates.

Flowers are diurnal, opening for about 5 hours during the day. This day-blooming trait links it to the next genus, *Lobivia;* some are so classified.

97

**LOBIVIA** (Cob Cacti) inhabits the highlands of Peru, Bolivia, and Argentina. The cacti included in this genus are similar to, and were once classified as Echinopsis; they differ only in being smaller, day-flowering, and in having a shorter floral tube.

The stems, globular to short-cylindric in form, are either solitary or branched at the base to form small clumps. The ribs are always distinct, from 10 to 50 or more, often wavy or broken into tubercles. The areoles are usually very spiny, in some species so much so that they hide the stem.

Flower buds arise on the sides of the stem from old areoles on growth of the previous seasons, in some species from near the apex, in others near the base. Flowers are diurnal, funnel-form to bell-shaped, with a short broad tube. As in Echinopsis, the tube bears scales with long hairs in the axils, and the small globular fruits split on one side when ripe.

**L. AUREA** (golden) Golden Cob Cactus, contains the forms of *Echinopsis aurea* that have the shorter flower-tubes. Stems are similar, globular to cylindric, with 14 to 15 sharp-edged ribs and clusters of yellowish-brown spines in the areoles. Flowers are short-funnelform, glossy, lemon-yellow to golden.

**L. HERTRICHIANA** (for William Hertrich, 1878-1966, Curator, Huntington Botanic Gardens) Scarlet Cob Cactus, a densely-clumping species from SE Peru, has glossy light green globular stems to 4 inches wide, with 11 acute ribs. The ribs are notched above the areoles with spreading yellow spines.

**L. FAMATIMENSIS** (of renown) Orange Cob Cactus, is native to N Argentina. The small oval stem elongates to 6 inches with age, and carries about 20 tuberculate ribs that tend to spiral around the stem. Short yellow spines fill the areoles. Flowers vary in color from yellowish to a deep red.

**L. BACKEBERGII** (for Curt Backeberg, 1894-1966, German cactus collector) Carmine Cob Cactus, grows on the Altiplano near La Paz, Bolivia, at 11,000 feet elevation. The plants are small globes 2 inches in diameter, with 15 spiraled notched ribs. The red petals have a bluish sheen.

**REBUTIA** (Crown Cacti), from the mountains of Peru, Bolivia, Argentina, and Chile, are small mostly clump-forming cacti with globose to short-cylindric stems; they resemble small Mammillarias (pp. 103-111) in that the unribbed stems are covered by spirals of nipples. Areoles are at the tips of these tubercles, filled with clusters of 8 to 40 mostly short needle-like spines. There are about 35 recognized species.

Flower buds arise from old tubercles at the base or side of the stem; the diurnal flowers are small, funnel-shaped, and very beautiful. They close in the evening and open again the next morning for several days in succession. The fruits are small berries covered by persistent withered scales.

**R. SENILIS** (old, white-haired) Fire Crown, from N Argentina and Chile, forms clumps of bluish flattened globes covered with clusters of white to yellowish interlocking spines. It has many horticultural forms, all based on flower colors.

**R. PSEUDODEMINUTA** (deceptively resembling *R. deminuta*) Red-Gold Crown, from N Argentina and S Bolivia, makes clumps of little 2-inch grass-green globes with prominent tubercles set with 2-3 central and 11 radial spines, glassy-white tipped by brown.

**R. KUPPERIANA** (for Prof. Kupper, Munich Botanic Garden) Scarlet Crown, from Bolivia, blooms freely from April to August; even blooms as a tiny 1-inch plant. Stems are small globes with sharp-pointed tubercles set in about 20 spirals.

**R. VIOLACIFLORA** (with violet-colored flowers) Violet Crown, from the Andes of Argentina and Bolivia at 9,000 feet elevation, is a tiny flattened globe less than an inch across, dense with 20-25 spirals of tubercles. It does not clump.

**R. PSEUDOMINUSCULA** (deceptively resembling *R. minuscula*) Crimson Crown, of the Argentine Andes at 9,000 feet elevation, forms clumps of small globes, each under 2 inches wide, with 12-16 spirals of dark green tubercles flushed with red.

**R. MINUSCULA** (very small) Red Crown, from NW Argentina, forms tufts of 2-inch flattened globes covered by low tubercles in 16-20 spirals. The flowers are freely borne from February to April; individual flowers last several days.

**CHAMAECEREUS** is a monotypic genus from the Andes in Tucumán Province, Argentina, with cylindric creeping stems with a few low ribs; it branches from near the base and forms small clumps. Flowers arise singly at lateral areoles on the old growth of preceding years. The globular fruits are dry and woolly.

**C. SILVESTRII** (for Argentine zoologist Philip Silvestri) Peanut Cactus, has soft fleshy finger-like joints 2-4 inches long and ½-inch thick, with 6-9 low tuberculate ribs. The tiny felted areoles carry clusters of 10-16 thin bristle-like spines that radiate in all directions.

Bell-shaped diurnal flowers appear in early spring; the tube is covered by scales that bear tufts of dark hair in the axils.

When grafted on *Pereskia aculeata* stock (p. 11), joints grow to over 12 inches in length and ¾-inch thick, and hundreds of branches develop.

**MAMMILLARIA** (Fishhook or Pincushion Cacti), with 100 or more valid species, ranges from California to western Oklahoma, then southward over Mexico into Central America; a few are native to the Antilles and the arid north coasts of Colombia and Venezuela. Fourteen species are indigenous to the United States.

Mammillarias are small plants with solitary or clustered stems, when mature they are globose, oval, cylindric, or turnip-shaped. Most are 1-4 inches tall and 1-3 inches wide, but a few grow to 12 inches high and 8 wide. The stem surface is covered by distinct separate tubercles with spine-bearing areoles at the tips; the spines are smooth, with a broad range of colors. Central spines, if present, may be straight, curved, or hooked, to 1 inch long in some; the shorter needle-like radials, 10-80 per areole, are straight.

Flower buds are formed on the old growth of previous seasons, and are located below the stem apex. They originate down between the tubercles, never from the spine-bearing areoles at their tips, nor are they obviously connected to the tubercles in any way. They arise from spine- or wool-bearing areoles on the stem between the tubercles.

Flowers are diurnal, usually bell-shaped, mostly small, from ¼-inch to 1 inch across, in a few species to 2 inches broad. They open in the forenoon, and close in the afternoon of the same day, but may open and close in this way for 2 or 3 successive days.

The small fleshy fruits, from ¼-inch to an inch long, are globular to elongate. They are smooth-skinned, without scales or other surface appendages, and do not split or open when ripe.

Some species hold thick milky latex in their stems; all other cacti have colorless watery sap.

**MAMMILLARIA LONGIMAMMA** (long-nippled), found from Hidalgo, Mexico to S Texas, has spherical 4-inch stems that branch to form clumps. The cylindrical 2-inch tubercles are tipped by 4-15 radiating spines. The large 2-inch flowers often appear in 3's. Many varieties are known.

**M. GEMINISPINA** (twin-spined), of north-central Mexico, develops beautiful dome-shaped clumps of 50 or more stems if planted out-of-doors. Axils of the conical tubercles are woolly; their tips bear 16-20 short white bristly radial spines and 2-4 black-tipped centrals 1 inch long. Flowers in fall.

**M. LASIACANTHA** (rough-spined) lives with only the top of its 1-inch stem above the limestone hills and mesas in desert and grasslands at 3000-4300 feet elevation. White spines, 50-80 per areole, hide the stems. It ranges from N Chihuahua into S New Mexico and the Big Bend.

**M. MICROCARPA** (small-fruited) Fishhook Cactus, has 1 principal hooked central spine per areole, a few shorter straight centrals, and 18-28 straight spreading radials. The stems, to 6 inches high and 2 wide, form clumps. It ranges from central Arizona to northern Sonora.

**MAMMILLARIA GUMMIFERA** (bearing gum) Biznaga de Chilitos; Coral Cactus, with numerous botanical varieties, ranges from N Mexico into Arizona, New Mexico, and Texas. It and its varieties are the only native U.S. cacti with milky latex in the tubercles. The fruits resemble chilis.

**M. GUMMIFERA** var. **MEIACANTHA** (smaller-spined), from Arizona, New Mexico, and Texas W of the Pecos, prefers stony soils of limestone origin. Its stems are usually unbranched hemispheres to 6 inches across, covered by hundreds of pyramid-like tubercles unhidden by the spines.

**M. POTTSII** (for John Potts, an American mining engineer who also collected cacti), from the Big Bend, Texas, and NE Mexico, lives in gravelly areas in the desert at 2500-3000 feet elevation. It sometimes forms small clumps; stems are cylindric, to 4 inches tall, and up to 1¾ inches in diameter.

**M. PROLIFERA** (forming off-shoots) var. **TEXANA** (of Texas) grows in the grasslands of NE Mexico and S Texas. Its little stems, to 3 inches high and an inch wide, clump to form mounds. Areoles have 8-10 dark-tipped central spines, and 30-60 white hair-like curly radials.

**MAMMILLARIA DIOICA** (dioecious, i.e., individual plants have unisexual flowers), from both the coast and desert of NW Baja California and SW California, forms clumps of cylindric stems 4-6 inches high. Flower color varies from yellow to white; petal midribs may be purplish or rose. Central spines are hooked.

**M. MACRACANTHA** (long-spined), from San Luis Potosi, Mexico, is a flattened globe in age, about 3 inches high and 6 wide, with large pyramidal tubercles armed with just 1 or 2 curved angled spines per areole; in the wild they elongate to 2 inches, but not in "captive" plants.

**M. MAINIAE** (for Mrs. F. M. Main, who first collected it, near Nogales, Mexico) grows in desert or grassland at 2000-4000 feet elevation, from Sinaloa, Mexico, to S-central Arizona. The one hooked central spine per areole is placed so the hooks are all turned counter-clockwise.

**M. TETRANCISTRA** (four-spined, referring to the hooked black central spines, generally 4 in number) California Fishhook Cactus, lives in sandy deserts at 450-2400 feet elevation, in S California, S Nevada, SW Utah, and W Arizona. Its seeds are half-covered by a corky aril nearly as big as the seed.

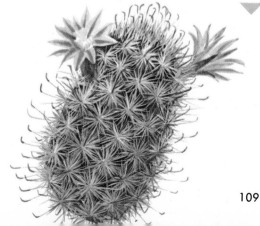

Although a great many species, varieties, and forms of Mammillaria have been described, the basic structure or morphology of their stems, flowers, and fruits is very much alike among all of them. The differences between them lie in the size, shape, and color of the plants and their parts, and in the arrangement and number of their spines. They are all neat compact plants with a symmetry that delights the eye. The spines, beautifully colored and arranged in intricate patterns, vie with the circle of bright flowers and fruits. These four species illustrate how strikingly their superficial appearance can vary.

**MAMMILLARIA ELONGATA** (elongated) Golden Stars; Gold Lace Cactus; Lady's-Finger, from E Mexico, branches from the base to form small dense clumps of delicate slender finger-like stems up to 4 inches long but scarcely more than ½-inch thick. Tubercles, arranged in only a few spirals, are tipped by a star-like cluster of down-curved yellow spines that interlock with those from adjacent tubercles, hiding the stem in gold lace.

**M. CANDIDA** (white-hairy) Snowball Cactus, from the state of San Luis Potosi, central Mexico, when young is a single little sphere hidden beneath the white spines. When older and about 2 inches wide it branches to form small clumps, and the stem elongates a bit. Areoles at the tips of the tubercles have over 50 horizontal bristly spines and 8-12 stouter porrect central spines often tipped with brown.

**M. PLUMOSA** (feathery) Feather Cactus, an unbelievable species from northern Mexico, has small much-branched stems that form dense clumps up to 10 inches across, completely hidden by the "feathers." This is the only cactus known in which the individual spines (40 per areole) are divided or feathered. They are weak and rub off easily if handled. In the city the plumes soon become a dirty gray unless grown under an inverted jar.

**M. BOMBYCINA** (silky, referring to the sheen on the spines) Silky Pincushion, from Coahuila, Mexico, is at first globular, becoming cylindric in age, forming huge clumps. The stems are up to 8 inches tall and 2 wide; the axils of the short conical tubercles are filled with dense tufts of white wool, especially near the crown of the plant. Areoles have 4 hooked central spines and 30-40 spreading radials.

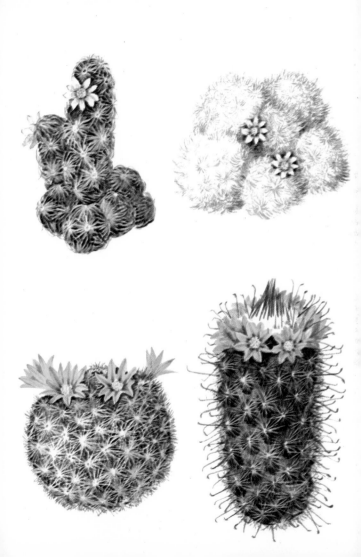

**GYMNOCALYCIUM** (Chin Cacti) is a South American genus found east of the Andes, mostly in northern Argentina, but also in Bolivia, Paraguay, Uruguay, and southern Brazil; a few range south into Patagonia. Most grow in grassland at no great altitude, although a few species range up to 10,000 feet.

Chin cacti are mostly small globular plants, solitary or clumping, with 5 to 32 tuberculate ribs. The tubercles have a "chin" or swelling just below the areole. Some species have large tubercles that crowd out of line, making the ribs hard to distinguish.

Flower buds arise in the spine-bearing areoles, in most species on new growth near the stem apex, in a few laterally from old areoles. The funnelform flowers have broad scales on the tube and ovary; there are no hairs, bristles, or spines on flowers or fruits.

Individual plants and clones of most species are self-sterile, and hybrids abound in this genus.

**G. SCHICKENDANTZII** (for Federico Schickendantz, Argentine botanist, 1837-1896) White Chin, of northern Argentina, is usually a solitary stem to 4 inches wide on which the tubercles coalesce into 7 broad ribs. Flowers, often borne by old and new areoles, are white, becoming pinkish as they age.

**G. MIHANOVICHII** (for a sailor, Mihanovich) Plaid Cactus, from the Chaco Boreal of Paraguay, is usually less than 2 inches wide, solitary, with 8 prominent sharp grayish-green ribs, often with horizontal bands of a contrasting color. Its flowers vary from pale yellow to brownish-green.

**G. DAMSII**, Dam's Chin, from northern Paraguay, is a solitary green globe, sometimes somewhat flattened, with 10 tuberculate ribs and straight short spreading spines, all radials. Its 2-inch white flowers are often tinged with pink; the fruits, an inch long and half as wide, are red when ripe.

**G. PLATENSE** (for Río de la Plata, near which it was first collected), ranges over most of Argentina, but is nearly extinct in the vicinity of the river. The plants, 3-inch flattened globes with 8-12 broad low ribs, grow half-hidden in the soil. Stem color may be blue-green, purple, or bronze.

**GYMNOCALYCIUM LEEANUM** (for the Messrs. Lee of Hammersmith Nurseries, W London, first to grow it in Europe), from Uruguay and Argentina, is a green globe with 9-11 broad ribs divided into 6-sided tubercles. Clump-forming, the new stems on slender stolons quickly put down roots.

**G. GIBBOSUM** (gibbous, referring to the prominent "chins"), from Argentina, is spherical when young, but cylindric in age, up to 8 inches tall. Its solitary stems have 12-14 tuberculate ribs. There are many varieties of this species, most of them self-pollinating. They vary in spine number and color.

**G. DENUDATUM** (naked, referring to the relatively few spines) Spider Cactus, from S Brazil, N Uruguay, and adjacent Argentina, is a partly flattened globe 2-6 inches wide, the tubercles coalesced into 5-8 broad low ribs. Its common name derives from the 5-8 curved spidery spines.

**G. SAGLIONE,** from the Andean region of NW Argentina, is the largest Gymnocalycium known; its solitary globular stems reach 15 inches across. Stems have 13-32 ribs, depending on the size of the plant, divided into large rounded tubercles. Only larger older plants flower.

**FEROCACTUS** (Barrel Cacti), with 20 to 30 species, is found from California to Texas, then southward in western Mexico and on the Mexican Plateau.

Ferocacti are normally unbranched; their stems are either flattened globes, ovals, or cylinders, from 6 inches to 10 feet high, and from 2 inches to 2 feet thick. They have from 13 to 30 ribs, composed of almost completely coalescent tubercles, with nearly circular to elliptic areoles.

The spines, in a multitude of colors, may be smooth or with cross-ribs. Areoles normally have 4 central spines, rarely 1 or 8, up to 6½ inches long, which can be needle-like or flattened, and either straight, curved, or hooked. Radial spines, 6 to 20 per areole, are ⅜ to 3 inches long, either straight or curved.

Flower buds form on new growth of the present season near the stem apex. Buds emerge from the top of the tubercles in a felted area next to and merging with the spine-bearing part of the areole; when the fruit falls it leaves a scar lasting for many years. The flowers, from 1½ to 3 inches wide, have a short tube shaped like an inverted cone.

The fruits, under 2 inches long, are fleshy and covered by broad rounded scales; the withered flower tube remains attached to them. They open when ripe by a short crosswise or lengthwise slit.

**F. WISLIZENII** (for Dr. F. A. Wislizenus, 1810-1889, St. Louis physician and explorer of the southwest) Candy, Southwestern, or Fishhook Barrel, is native in the Arizona and Chihuahuan deserts at 1000-5600 feet elevation but restricted to areas receiving summer rains. Its massive stems are 2-10 feet tall and 1-2 feet thick, with 20-28 ribs. It flowers profusely in summer.

The spines burn fiercely like a torch; Texas cowboys so often used it for bonfires that the state ordered a penalty of $50 for each cactus so burned.

**FEROCACTUS COVILLEI** (for F. V. Coville, 1867-1937, American botanist and Curator, U.S. National Herbarium) Traveler's-Compass; Hermosillo; Coville's Barrel, from S Arizona and adjacent Sonora, Mexico, has barrel-shaped or cylindric stems 2-8 feet high and 1-2 feet thick, with 20-30 ribs.

The central spine, 3-4 inches long, is strongly cross-ribbed, flat on its upper surface, hooked or strongly curved at the tip; these spines were used by the Indians for fishhooks.

This and some other barrel cacti all lean to the southwest as they grow, earning them the name "Traveler's-Compass."

**F. ACANTHODES** (acanthus-like) California Barrel, is a desert plant, usually a single column 3-10 feet tall and 1 foot thick, with 18-27 ribs. Its central spines are un-hooked, the lowest 3-6 inches long; it grows in gravel or rock at 200-2000 feet elevation in Baja and SE California.

In var. *lecontei*, of Sonora, SE California, S Nevada, SW Utah and W Arizona, the longest central spine is 2-3 inches; it grows mostly at 2500-5000 feet, but at 1000-3000 in part of Arizona.

Var. *eastwoodiae*, of rocky ledges at 1300-3800 feet in S Arizona, has yellow spines.

119

**ECHINOCACTUS** (Barrel Cacti), a genus with about 12 species, ranges from California to Texas, and south to Querétaro, central Mexico.

Some Echinocacti have solitary stems, others branch to form clumps. Mature stems vary from 2 inches to 2 feet tall, and from 2 inches to 1 foot thick, depending on the species. Most have 8 to 27 ribs formed by almost completely coalescent tubercles, with nearly circular to elliptic areoles.

Some species are spineless; if spiny, all of the spines are annulate. Central spines may be lacking; if present they are red, 1 to 4 per areole, straight or curved, needle-like or flattened, from 1 to 3 inches long. Radial spines, 5 to 11 per areole, are like the centrals but smaller, ¾ to 2 inches long.

Flowers and fruits are borne on new growth in the same way as in Ferocactus (p. 116), and the flowers are similar in form, from 1½ to 2¾ inches broad.

The fruits, to 2 inches long, are dry when ripe; they are scaly, with long hairs under the scales, sometimes hiding the fruit in a dense woolly coat.

Most Barrel Cacti in both genera grow very slowly. Growth may cease altogether during years of drought, to be resumed again when rain returns. Some can adsorb and store enough water during wet periods to last through the dry years.

**E. POLYCEPHALUS** (many-headed) of the Mojavean Desert, grows on rocky slopes or in clays in the deserts at 100-2500 feet elevation, in NW Sonora, SE California, S Nevada, and W Arizona.

This cactus forms clumps of 10-30 stems, the tallest in the center; the clumps are up to 2 feet high and 4 feet across. As its spines grow they are encased in a dense layer of gray felt that peels away in sheets.

Var. *xeranthemoides* grows at over 3800 feet on south-facing ledges, mostly in NW Arizona; its spines are not hairy.

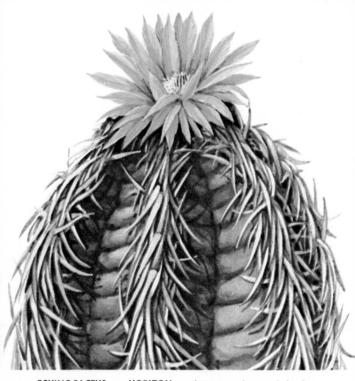

**ECHINOCACTUS HORIZON-THALONIUS** (having a horizontal body) Eagle Claws; Turk's Head; Devil's Head grows in limestone at 2100-6500 feet elevation, from Trans-Pecos Texas and S New Mexico to San Luis Potosi, Mexico.

The stems of this cactus vary from flattened globes to ovals or columns, from 6-12 inches tall and 4-6 inches across, with 7-13 flat ribs that are some-times cross-furrowed. Its 3 central spines, one of which curves downward, are pale gray or black on the surface, but red or red and yellow underneath. The radials, 5-8 per areole, curve slightly outward.

The flowers, over 2 inches in diameter, appear in June and July. Its fruits, first juicy but dry at maturity, are covered by soft white wool; they open by a pore at the tip.

**E. TEXENSIS** (of Texas) Horse Crippler; Manca Caballo; Devil's Head; Devil's Pincushion, grows from sea level up to 3650 feet, and ranges from SE New Mexico and most of Texas south across Coahuila, Nuevo Leon, and Tamaulipas in Mexico.

The stems of this plant are 5-8 inches high and to a foot wide, with 13-27 ribs. There is 1 central spine per areole, 2-3 inches long, curved rigidly downward, and usually 6 spreading unequal radials, from ½ to almost 2 inches long. All the spines are thick, heavy, and iron-hard; they have lamed many a steer in Texas, and cowboys uproot it whenever they see it.

The flowers, over 2 inches wide, appear from April to July; each one lasts 4 days, closing at night.

**NOTE:** These four species, greatly admired and widely grown, are actually little Barrel Cacti pertaining to the genus Echinocactus. When 3 of them were first discovered, they were described as species of Echinocactus (*E. ornatus* in 1828, *E. asterias* in 1845, and *E. capricornis* in 1851). The Belgian botanist Charles Lemaire first described the species *myriostigma* in 1839 and created the genus Astrophytum for it; he moved *E. asterias* to Astrophytum in 1868. But no botanists considered Lemaire's genus Astrophytum as valid (*A. myriostigma* was put into Echinocactus by Salm-Dyck in 1845) until 1922, when Britton and Rose revived it and also put the other 2 species there. Botanists now agree all 4 are Echinocacti.

**E. MYRIOSTIGMA** (with myriads of spots) Bishop's Cap, grows in oak and pine forests around San Luis Potosi, Mexico, at 7500 feet elevation. With a lens its spots are seen as tufts of short gray hairs. The globular stems, usually 5-ribbed and to 6 inches high, are 6, 8, or 10-ribbed and to 2 feet tall in some forms. Its diurnal blooms appear in May, June, or July.

**E. ASTERIAS** (starred) Sea Urchin Cactus; Star Cactus, of grassland or brushland at low elevations in Starr Co., Texas, Nuevo Leon, and Tamaulipas is always spineless. Its stem, usually only 1-3 inches tall and to 3 wide, is divided into 8 rounded segments separated by narrow grooves. Its tiny green or pink fruits are hidden in the wool of the areoles.

**E. CAPRICORNIS** (goat-horned) Goat's Horn Cactus, grows on the limestone and slate hills of Coahuila, Mexico. Young plants are flattened globes with 7-9 sharply-edged ribs; in age the stems elongate up to 10 inches. At least 6 varieties are recognized, based on diversity of the spines: some are almost spineless, others with bristles, one with 15-20 large coarse "goat horns" at each areole.

**E. ORNATUS** (ornate or adorned) Star Cactus, a desert species of Querétaro and Hidalgo, central Mexico, has solitary stems, globose when young but cylindric with age, with 8 prominent ribs. Some forms are reported to become 2 feet tall and a foot thick. The spreading awl-like spines, 5-11 per areole, are all radials. When ripe, the fruit opens at the top in the shape of a five-pointed star.

**STENOCACTUS** (Brain Cacti), with about 30 species closely related to Echinocactus, ranges from Hidalgo and Aguascalientes to Coahuila, Mexico.

Most are small solitary globular plants with 10 to 50 or 100 thin wavy ribs, giving them a wrinkled brain-like appearance. The areoles, often only 1 or 2 on each rib, have many unhooked, mostly papery flat spines that often hide the plant. The small flowers, on new growth as in Echinocactus, hold their petals erect or only partly expanded. The scales on the fruit have no hair or wool in their axils.

The slight differences between many of the described species makes it difficult to tell them apart.

**S. HASTATUS** (spear-spined), from Hidalgo, is a solitary flattened globe to 4 inches tall and 5 wide, with 35 congested steep wavy ribs; its areoles bear 5-6 short straight or slightly curved yellow radial spines, and 1 long broad upright spear-like central spine. Its fruits are dry at maturity.

**S. VIOLACIFLORUS** (with violet flowers), of Aguascalientes and Zacatecas, becomes columnar in age. The overlapping spines hide its 35 deeply wavy ribs.

**S. LLOYDII** (for F. E. Lloyd, who first collected it) is nearly globular, with 50 or more thin folded ribs. The flowers have two-cleft stigma lobes.

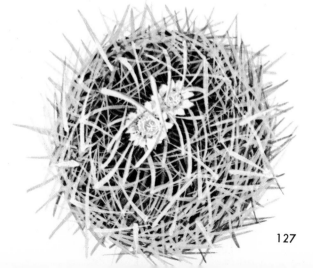

**NOTOCACTUS** (Ball Cacti) mostly grow in grassland at moderate altitudes; they are all South American, from south of the Equator, ranging from central Brazil and southern Peru to south-central Argentina.

The solitary or branched stems of young plants are spheres or flattened globes, in age columnar in some species. Mature stems vary from 2 inches to 6 feet tall, and from 2 to 20 inches thick, with 6 to over 60 vertical or spiraled ribs, the tubercles either almost completely coalescent or distinct. Areoles are felted and spiny; the spines, 3 to more than 40 per areole, vary from barely visible bristles to 3-inch awls or needles.

Flowers are from new growth in or near the center of the plant; they are short and broad, showy, with a scaly, bristly, and hairy flower-tube and ovary; the scales, with bristles, hairs, or dense wool in their axils, persist on the fruits.

**N. APRICUS** (early, referring to the May-June bloom) Sun Cup, of Uruguay, forms small clumps of flattened 2-inch globes, sunken or cupped at the apex, with 15-20 curved semi-tuberculate ribs densely covered with flexible interlocking spines. The proportionately huge flowers are 3 inches long and equally wide.

**N. PATAGONICUS** (of Patagonia) grows in barren pebbly washes or on rocky glacial deposits in the Chubut Valley of Argentina, usually as a slender erect cylinder to 2 feet high, rarely to 20 inches thick, with 6-10 straight or spiraled wavy ribs. Areoles are close-set, with some hooked central spines.

**N. MAMMULOSUS** (nippled), of Brazil, Uruguay, and Argentina, is a solitary 3-inch dark green or purplish sphere with 18-25 strongly nippled ribs almost hidden by the yellowish interlocking spines, 22-34 per areole. Its satiny yellow flowers with purple stigmas appear abundantly in June and July. The ovary is scaly.

**N. OTTONIS** (for Friedrich Otto, 1782-1856, German botanist) Indian Head, of Argentina, S Brazil, Uruguay, and Paraguay, has many varieties, all free-flowering from June to August. The irritable stamens wrap round the style in 3-6 seconds if blown on, rubbing pollen onto the stigma-lobes.

**NOTOCACTUS SCHUMANNIAN-US** (for Karl M. Schumann, 1851-1904, German cactologist) Citron Ball, from Paraguay and NE Argentina, is first solitary and globose, later elongating to 3 feet or more and becoming bent or lying down, 4 to 16 inches thick, with about 30 low sharp ribs.

**N. HASELBERGII** (for cactophile Dr. von Haselberg of Stralsund, Pomerania) Scarlet Ball, from Rio Grande do Sur, Brazil, is a solitary 5-inch globe with about 30 semi-tuberculate ribs, hidden by the silvery-white bristly radial spines. Flowers vary from orange to fiery red; they have 6 erect stigma-lobes.

**N. LENINGHAUSII**, Golden Ball, also from Rio Grande do Sur, is ready to flower and clump when a 4-inch sphere. Its 30 narrow ribs appear hazy under the soft golden down-pointing spines. It slowly becomes cylindric, to 10 inches high in 12-15 years; in old age to over 3 feet.

**N. SCOPA** (like a brush, referring to the spines) Silver Ball, of S Brazil and Uruguay, finally becomes an 18-inch column. The bristle-like radial spines, over 40 per areole, hide the 30-40 low rounded ribs. It has many forms, all based on spine color and arrangement. Stigma-lobes about 10, all red.

**PARODIA** grows mostly in open plains among scattered shrubs or long grasses for protection from the full sun, from northern Argentina to central Bolivia and southern Brazil, some at high altitudes.

These are small globular or elongate cacti, usually solitary, with straight or spiraled tuberculate ribs. Areoles crown the tubercles, and are especially spiny and woolly at the top of the plant; many of them have some hooked spines.

The diurnal flowers, large for the size of the plants, develop in areoles of new tubercles near the center of the stem, often 3 or more at once, and last several days. The ovary is scaly, usually with white wool and bristles in the scale axils. Fruits are small and dry, containing dust-like seed.

Over 100 species of Parodia have been described, many based on trivial differences; valid species probably number around thirty.

**P. MUTABILIS** (changeable, changing color), from the Andean foothills in Salta Province, Argentina, becomes slightly elongate, to 4 inches tall and 3 wide. Each areole is armed by 50 thin white radial spines and 4 stouter centrals arranged in the form of a cross, the longest one hooked.

**P. MAASSII**, Vermillion Parodia, of S Bolivia and N Argentina, is sometimes found in crevices in the rock at over 11,000 feet elevation. It is a yellow-green globe 4-6 inches tall; the 13 tuberculate ribs are prominent at the top of the stem, faint at the base. The 3-inch curved central spines may hook.

**P. AUREISPINA** (golden-spined) Tom Thumb Cactus, is common in cultivation but rare in Salta, Argentina, its native habitat, where it grows at altitudes of 9000 feet. This solitary globe seldom exceeds 3 inches, and begins flowering when less than an inch high. It also has hooks on some central spines.

**P. SANGUINIFLORA** (with blood-red flowers) Crimson Parodia, also from Salta, starts as a sphere, in age is a 4-5 inch cylinder 2 or 3 inches thick. The ribs are spirals of prominent conical tubercles, set with 15 bristly white radial spines and 4 brown centrals, the lowest hooked. The flowers have silky petals.

**MELOCACTUS** (Melon Cacti), of semi-arid locations, range from Cuba down the Antilles to Venezuela, Colombia, and Brazil, and from Mexico to Honduras.

Young Melocacti look like young Barrel Cacti, with 9 to 20 ribs and spiny areoles. But when old enough to bloom, the central flower-bearing areoles form a *cephalium* or "head," on top of the plant; it looks like a compact mass of hairs and bristles, but has a woody core. Once formed, it becomes a permanent feature of the stem, which is then full-sized.

The tiny flowers open in mid-afternoon on top of the cephalium; the club-shaped fruits are edible.

**M. MELOCACTOIDES** (resembling a Melocactus) Cabeça de Frade, is common on thin soils of rocky outcrops from Pernambuco to Rio de Janeiro, Brazil. It is typical of the smaller species, its stems to 4 inches high and 6 wide, with 10 broad ribs, awl-shaped spines, and a small neat cephalium.

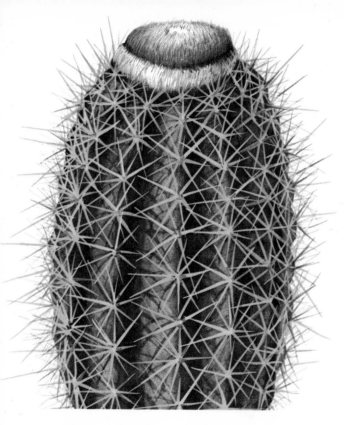

**M. INTORTUS** (twisted, referring to the ribs, which are slightly spiraled in some specimens) Turk's Cap, is found from the southern Bahamas to Dominica; it is a barrel-like cactus to over 3 feet high, with 14-20 thick deep ribs armed by 10-15 long stout spines per areole. In age its cephalium becomes tall and cylindric, making it look like a Turkish fez; the Turk's Islands take their name from this plant, and depict it on their postage stamps.

In its middle range, from the Mona Passage to the Virgin Islands, the plants show much variation in their spines from one island to another.

**SCLEROCACTUS**, 6 species, ranges from southeastern California to northern Utah, western Colorado, northwestern New Mexico, and northern Arizona.

Sclerocacti are usually solitary, the stems either flattened globes, ovals, or cylinders, from 2 to 16 inches high and 1 to 6 inches wide. Their 12 to 17 ribs are formed of tubercles that coalesce for half to four-fifths of the height of the ribs.

Areoles are armed by complex spines, all smooth and without cross-ridges. Centrals, if present, 1 to 11 per areole, usually of 2 or 3 kinds, one or more often hooked, exasperating to dislodge if touched. The 6 to 15 shorter radials are needle-like or flattened.

Flowers are from the new growth as in the genus Echinocactus (p. 120), short-funnelform, about 1 to 2 inches broad, and diurnal. The fruits are dry when ripe, naked or with a few scales, with an apical cup hidden by the persistent withered flower-tube.

**S. MESAE-VERDAE** (of Mesa Verde, Colorado) Mesa Verde Cactus, is one of our rarest cacti, adapted to extremely alkaline soil and extreme aridity, found only in the corners of SW Colorado and NW New Mexico. The tubercles, separate on young plants, coalesce into 13-17 ribs as the plants age and grow larger.

**S. WHIPPLEI** (for A. W. Whipple, 1816-1863, Lt., U. S. Army), var. *Roseus* (rosy) grows in sand and gravel near the major watercourses in the lower Navajoan Desert at 3500-6700 feet elevation, in SE Utah, W Colorado, and N Arizona. Cylindric in age. To 6 inches tall, 2½ inches thick; flowers purple, pink, or white.

**S. POLYANCISTRUS** (many-spined), of the Mojavean Desert at 2500-7000 feet, California and S Nevada, is shaped like a 6-inch pineapple. Its 13-17 ribs, on which only the tubercle tips are free, are barely visible under the formidable spines. All but 1 or 2 of the 9-11 long central spines per areole are hooked.

**S. WHIPPLEI** var. **INTERMEDIUS** (intermediate) Devil's Claw, is the commonest variety, ranging from E Utah and W Colorado to N Arizona and NW New Mexico, at 3500-7000 feet elevation, withstanding minus 20° F. Its stems are mostly 3-8, inches long, 2-4 thick. Flowers are purple, pink, or white.

**PEDIOCACTUS**, with 7 species, is found in the mountains of the Columbia River Basin and the Great Basin, in the Rockies, and on the Colorado Plateau, but 6 of the 7 are restricted to limited areas within this vast range. Four of them were recently discovered.

The stems vary from flattened globes to cylinders, from ½ to 6 inches tall, and from ⅜ to 6 inches thick, but most are very small. The stems are ribless, covered with spirally-arranged tubercles, the areoles at their tips. The spines tend to hide the stems; they are extremely diverse in color, number per areole, length, texture, posture, and flatness.

The diurnal flowers are from areoles on new tubercles near the center of the plant; they are small, from ⅖ to 1 inch broad. The tiny fruits, dry when ripe, are naked or with a few scales, with a shallow apical cup, opening round the top and down one side.

**P. SIMPSONII** is the wide-ranging species, from E Oregon, S Idaho, and S Wyoming to W South Dakota; and across W-central Nevada to N Arizona and N New Mexico. It prefers fine dry soils high in the Rockies, at 6000-9500 feet in sunny locations. Its stems are mostly 1-5 inches high.

**P. SILERI** (for A. L. Siler, who collected cacti for botanical study) grows in the Navajoan and Mojavean Deserts of SW Utah and NW Arizona at 4700-5000 feet elevation. Its solitary stem is 2-5 inches high, 2-4 thick, with dense spines. Areoles have 3-7 porrect central spines about an inch long, and 11-15 radials.

**P. PEEBLESIANUS** (for Robert H. Peebles, 1900-1956, American botanist) is a tiny globe to 1 inch high, often pulled down into the ground in dry weather with only the top showing. The typical plants lack central spines, have 3-5 radials, and are known only from Navajo County, Arizona.

**P. PAPYRACANTHUS** (paper-spined) Grama-Grass Cactus, grows on open flats in woodlands and grasslands in E-central Arizona and W New Mexico at 5000-7300 feet. Its solitary finger-like stem, 1-3 inches tall and less than an inch thick, grow unseen in or near grama grass; its flat spines mimic the dry grass.

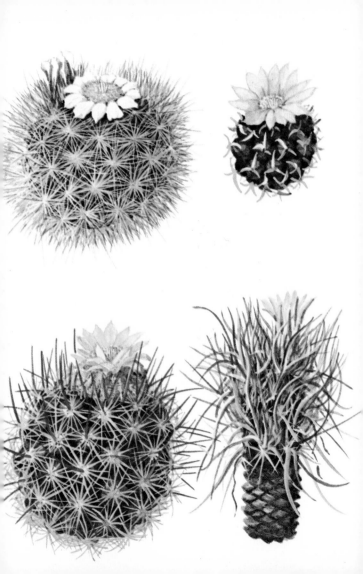

**THELOCACTUS** contains a few Mexican species that range from Chihuahua to Tamaulipas, south to Hidalgo in central Mexico; one of them crosses the border into southern Texas.

Thelocacti are solitary or clustered, in form hemispherical to long-oval, 3 to 6 inches high, 2 to 8 inches wide, mostly with 8 to 12 ribs divided into large, often spiraled, tubercles. The nearly circular areoles at the tubercle tips are armed with 4 to 21 spines (14 centrals, 3-17 radials).

Flower buds appear on the new growth near the center of the plant, from the upper side of the tubercle next to the spine-bearing part of the areole. Flowers are diurnal, bell-shaped, mostly showy, to over 2 inches across. The fruits are dry when ripe, with from 5 to 20 scales; the withered flower-tube remains attached to them. They open at the base by a diagonal slit or pore.

**T. LEUCACANTHUS** (white-spined), from NW Hidalgo, is a clump-forming species with short-cylindric stems 4-6 inches tall. Its 8-13 ribs, sometimes spiraled, are composed of blunt-ended tubercles. Areoles have a lone 2-inch dark central spine and 7-20 short radials, yellow when young, but gray in age.

**T. NIDULANS** (nest-like) Bird's Nest Cactus, of Coahuila, is a hemisphere to 4 inches high, but up to 8 wide. The tubercles are nearly separate, the ribs indistinct. Its small spines weather away, leaving 4-6 larger ones at each areole; these fray into wool, and the plant looks nest-like.

**T. FOSSULATUS** (channeled or dimpled, referring to the tips of the tubercles), from San Luis Potosi, grows at about 7000 feet elevation. The stem is globose or flattened, to 6 inches wide. Its large flabby bronze-green tubercles are dimpled. The sunken areoles have 1 long central spine, 4-5 unequal radials.

**T. BICOLOR** (two-colored, referring to the flower) Glory of Texas, grows from central Mexico to S Texas, where 2 varieties occur: var. *schottii*, with the 4 central spines keeled, to 1¾ inches long, and with 15-17 radials; and var. *flavidispinus*, its centrals under 1 inch long, with only 12-14 radials.

**NEOLLOYDIA**, with some 12 to 15 species, ranges from Death Valley in SE California to Texas, southward to northern Sonora and to San Luis Potosi.

These are small, sometimes clump-forming cacti with oval to cylindric stems, mostly 2 to 6 inches high, rarely to 15 inches, and from 1 to 5 inches thick, covered by separate or nearly separate tubercles. The circular areoles at their tips are armed with 1 to 8 central and 3 to 32 radial spines, all straight, in an array of colors.

Flower buds appear on new growth near the center of the stem from a felted area on the upper side of the tubercle, located some distance from the spine-bearing areole but connected to it by an isthmus that runs along the whole tubercle; it forms a long narrow persistent scar after shedding the fruit. Flowers are 1 to 3 inches broad. The scaly dry fruits either open at the base, or by 1 to 3 lengthwise slits.

**N. CONOIDEA** (cone-like) grows on limestone from central Mexico to Brewster, Pecos, and Terrell Counties, Texas. Its green stems may form dense clumps. Stems are to 4 inches high and 2 wide; tubercles tend to organize into ribs. The areoles mostly carry 4 dark central spines and 15-28 radials.

**N. INTERTEXTA** (interwoven, referring to the spines) White Viznagita, grows on limestone in grasslands at 3900-5000 feet, from SE Arizona to the Texas Big Bend, and also in Chihuahua and Sonora. Upper centrals and all radial spines are flattened against the stem; lower centrals are porrect.

**N. MARIPOSENSIS** (for the Mariposa (quicksilver) Mine, in SW Brewster Co., Texas, near which it was first discovered) grows on limestone in the desert at 2400-3300 feet, also in Presidio Co., Texas, and in Coahuila. The tubercles coalesce at the base; young plants have 13 ribs, old ones 21.

**N. JOHNSONII** (for Joseph Ellis Johnson, 1817-1882, amateur Utah botanist) Pink Viznagita, of the Mojavean Desert, from Death Valley to S Nevada, SW Utah, and W Arizona, grows 4-6 inches tall and 2-4 wide; old plants may reach 10 inches. Its flowers vary from magenta to yellow-green.

**ANCISTROCACTUS**, with 4 species in S Texas or Mexico, is distinct: In older plants, the tubercle bases coalesce into ribs; areoles of young stems have 1 central spine, of old stems 3-4, the lower hooked, as may be some of the lower 6-22 radials. The first flowers, from new tubercles near the stem tip, are adjacent to the spiny part of the areole; in later years nearer and nearer the base of new tubercles, but connected to the areole by a groove. The juicy fruits do not open.

**A. TOBUSCHII** (for H. Tobusch, who discovered it in 1951) grows on limestone at about 1500 feet in Bandera Co., Texas. Only a few hundred plants are known to exist.

**A. SCHEERI** (For Frederick Scheer 1792-1868, German botanist) is found at low elevations from Val Verde to Jim Wells and Hidalgo Cos., Texas, and in NE Mexico.

**LOPHOPHORA**, a monotypic genus, grows on limestone or lime soils in desert or scrub at 500-4000 feet, from near the Rio Grande in Texas to Querétaro, Mexico. Stems are solitary or clumping, hemispheres or short cylinders, 1-3 inches high, 2-4 wide, with 5-13 tuberculate ribs. Mature plants are spineless. The flowers form at the tip of new tubercles at the center of the stem, next to the woolly part of the areole. The bare fruits are red and fleshy.

**L. WILLIAMSII**, Peyote, is like a huge carrot with only a button-like top above ground. The dry tops, or "Mescal Buttons," contain powerful hallucinogenic alkaloids; its psychoactivity was known to many Indian peoples in pre-Colombian times, to whom it is sacred, with supernatural therapeutic powers; it is bowed to in reverence when passing it in the field.

**CORYPHANTHA** (Pincushion Cacti), with between 20 and 30 species, ranges from Alberta, Canada, to central Mexico. Fourteen species are native in the United States, ranging from Oregon to Minnesota, south to southern California and western Louisiana.

These small ribless tuberculate cacti superficially resemble Mammillarias (pp. 105-111), and are confused with them. Coryphantha differs as follows:

The central spines, 1-10 or more per areole, can be straight, curved, hooked, or twisted; in size and form they shade into the 5-40 usually straight radials.

Flowers are on new growth of the current season, near the stem apex; in mature stems, they originate at the base of the upper side of the tubercle, but are connected to the spine-bearing part of the areole by a narrow felted groove. On young stems, the buds appear halfway up the side of the tubercle. Tubercles of plants too young to flower are not grooved.

**C. MINIMA** (smallest or least) is known only from the hills of Brewster Co., Texas, where it grows at altitudes of 4000-4300 feet. Its solitary or few-branched stems, up to an inch long and half as wide, have some 20 spines per areole, all lying against the stem, the innermost thick, with sharp tips.

**C. MACROMERIS** (with large parts, referring to the tubercles) Long Mamma, grows in clay or gravel in the desert at 2600-4300 feet, from S New Mexico and W of the Pecos in Texas, to Zacatecas, Mexico. The plants cluster by budding new stems in the grooves of lower tubercles.

**C. SCHEERI** (for Frederick Scheer 1792-1868, German botanist), Needle Mulee, with several varieties, ranges from SE Arizona to the Davis Mountains of Texas, and to N Sonora and Chihuahua. Stems are large for the genus, to 7 inches tall and to 4 thick. It flowers from April to July.

**C. MACROMERIS** var. **RUNYONII** (for Robert Runyon, who first collected it, in 1921) Dumpling Cactus grows on gravel or white silt at low elevations in extreme S Texas and adjacent Mexico. It forms clumps up to 18 inches wide, of stems that originate from the top of the taproots.

**CORYPHANTHA SULCATA** (grooved lengthwise, referring to the tubercles) Pineapple Cactus, of S-central Texas and Nuevo Leon, Mexico, grows among junipers, oaks, and shrubs on limestone hills, and is not a strict desert species. It quickly forms dense clumps of new stems which bud from the grooves of old tubercles; these low uneven clumps become over 2 feet broad. Individual adult stems are usually flattened, to 3 inches thick but seldom that high. Ripe fruits are green.

**C. VIVIPARA** (sprouting from the parent, referring to the many offshoots) Spiny Star, with its varieties, is found from Oregon and Alberta to Minnesota, south to S California, Kansas, Oklahoma, Texas, New Mexico, and Arizona. It may form clumps a foot high and over 2 feet wide of more than 200 stems. The 1 to 2-inch flowers in some varieties open on just 1 or 2 days of the year, others bloom several times in a season. Flowers vary from pink to red, lavender, or yellow.

**C. STROBILIFORMIS** (cone-like) inhabits limestone of deserts or grasslands at 2500-5100 feet, from SE Arizona to the Big Bend Region of Texas, and south into Chihuahua. Its stems, solitary or in small clumps, are 2-8 inches high, 1-2 wide; the spines almost hide the stem. Tubercles are crowded and turn upward, overlapping each other, like the segments of a pine cone. Old stems, unlike most species, hold the basal tubercles; these harden and lose their spines.

**C. MISSOURIENSIS** (of Missouri, but referring to the River, on the high hills of which it was discovered) Missouri Pincushion ranges widely over grasslands and shrubby hills of the Great Plains, from Montana to Manitoba and Minnesota, south to Arizona and NW Louisiana. Its young spines are pubescent, covered by tiny white hairs visible with a lens. The crimson fruits take nearly a year to ripen, and are often seen on the plant with its early May flowers.

149

**CORYPHANTHA RAMILLOSA** (having many branches, a misnomer) grows on limestone in the desert at 2460-3440 feet elevation. Mainly of Coahuila, it ranges north into Brewster and Terrell Cos., Texas. The nearly spherical stem is usually solitary or only sparingly branched, with flattened tubercles that overlap upward. Areoles have 4 principal and 3 accessory needle-like central spines, and 9-20 flattened curving twisted radials.

**C. SNEEDII** (for J. R. Sneed, who discovered it) grows on limestone ledges in desert and grass at 4260-5400 feet on the Franklin Mountains, between Las Cruces, New Mexico, and El Paso, Texas. Never common, it is almost extinct in its native site from indiscriminate collecting. This little cactus makes dense clumps of 100 or more stems; like C. *strobiliformis* (p. 149), the basal tubercles are retained and become hard, losing their spines.

150

**C. ROBERTII** (for Robert Runyon, who discovered it) Junior Tom Thumb Cactus, also prefers limestone of desert or grassland at about 1000 feet elevation; it ranges from NE Mexico into the Rio Grande Valley from Val Verde to Hidalgo Cos., Texas. Its little spiny stems, seldom more than 2 inches high and under an inch thick, quickly branch to form large low irregular clumps, so similar to the rock and grass about them that they are hard to see.

**C. CORNIFERA** (bearing horns) var. **ECHINUS** (spined) grows on desert limestone at 2160-4600 feet, from Chihuahua and Coahuila to El Paso, Howard, Coke, and Val Verde Cos., Texas. Young stems are spherical and solitary, elongating to 2 or 3 inches and forming clumps of 3-6 stems. Areoles have 3-4 central spines, one an inch long and porrect; the 16-26 radials lie flat against the stem and interlock with those of adjacent areoles.

151

**AZTEKIUM**, a monotypic genus, was discovered in Nuevo Leon, Mexico, in 1929, but has since also been found in Guatemala. The ribs are much furrowed and folded. The flowers arise from the center of the plant, often several at once, have only a few stamens, with the stigma and style no taller than the stamens.

**A. RITTERI** (for F. Ritter, well-known cactus collector) is tiny, just under 2 inches across when mature. The grooves and ridges of its 9 to 11 ribs have been likened to Aztec sculpture. The closely-set woolly areoles at the crown bear 1 to 3 short but stout spines which soon shed. The tiny pink fruit is hidden in the wool on the crown, and contains minute seeds.

When about 1 inch in diameter the plant is ready to flower and give rise to clumps. From then on its growth is slow. A day-bloomer: the Berlin Botanic Garden had a clump which opened 26 flowers all on the same day.

**OBREGONIA**, with one species, is native to northeastern Mexico. In character it is closely related to Leuchtenbergia (p. 154), and also shows affinities to Strombocactus (p. 155) and Ariocarpus (p. 156). It has a thick taproot, fleshy tubercles tipped by spiny areoles, and flowers from the youngest tubercles.

**O. DENEGRII** (for Sr. De Negri, who was Minister of Agriculture of Mexico at the time of its discovery) inhabits the limestone desert of the Llanos de Joumave, in SW Tamaulipas.

The stems are flattened globes, grayish to dark green, seldom over 2 inches high but to 3-5 inches wide, with leaf-like stiff 3-angled tubercles arranged in spirals, the whole plant looking rather like an artichoke. The Nahuatl Indians of Mexico also call this plant "Peyotl," and relate it in folklore and folk medicine to Peyote (p. 145); it is purported to contain hallucinogenic alkaloids and to be used similarly.

153

**LEUCHTENBERGIA**, a monotypic genus found from 4800 to 6000 feet elevation around San Luis Potosi, Hidalgo, Mexico, has a parsnip-like root, elongated finger-like tubercles with areoles at the tips, and twisted papery spines. Flowers are borne near the tip of young tubercles close to the center of the plant.

**L. PRINCIPIS** (for Eugene de Beauharnais, Prince of Eichstadt and Duke of Leuchtenberg, French statesman, 1781-1824) Agave Cactus. When growing, the plant spreads its tubercles widely apart, but in dry weather they are held erect and pressed together. Old plants form woody trunk-like bases by shedding the old tubercles, and offshoots may arise from their axils. In age plants can reach a height of 28 inches. The fragrant flowers are not shed, but remain at the tip of the olive-shaped gray scaly fruits. Agave Cactus has been hybridized with *Ferocactus acanthodes* (p. 119); the progeny are intermediate in character.

**STROMBOCACTUS,** also monotypic, has a strong turnip-like root, a small depressed globular stem covered with spirally-arranged overlapping tubercles, and a spine-bearing areole at the tip of each tubercle. Flowers arise from the new growth at the crown. The tiny seed are hard to distinguish with the naked eye.

**S. DISCIFORMIS** (shaped like a discus) grows on low crumbly shale ridges on the banks of dry washes in Querétaro, Mexico, in very arid desert. Old specimens occasionally become globose and as much as 8 inches tall. The spines calcify and are shed from the old hard scale-like tubercles near the base of the plant. The crown is slightly depressed and felted with white wool. The diurnal flowers appear in early spring; individual flowers stay open several days, and vary from white to pale yellow. The fruit splits lengthwise, exposing seed so small that if laid end to end 76 seeds are required to form a line just one inch long.

155

**ARIOCARPUS** contains six species of true mimicry plants almost the exact color of the soil in which they grow. They are unbranched, with thick carrot-like roots and a broad low top covered with overlapped but unfused tubercles. Flowers arise at the woolly base of new tubercles near the center of the plant.

**A. FISSURATUS** (fissured) Living Rock. Native to hot dry barren tablelands of southwestern Texas and northeastern Mexico at elevations from 1500 to 10,000 feet where rain seldom falls, these plants are easily mistaken for the weathered limestone in which they grow. The root contracts in the dry season and pulls the plant down into the soil. The tubercles have porous upper surfaces which permit absorption of dew, often the only moisture available. Growth is very slow. Flowering occurs from August to October; flowers appear singly or in 2's or 4's and remain open 3 or 4 days in succession. The seed remains viable for years.

# BIBLIOGRAPHY

Backeberg, Curt, DIE CACTACEAE; HANDBUCH DER KAKTEENKUNDE (6 Vols.), Gustav Fischer Verlag, Jena, 1958-1962

Benson, Lyman, THE CACTI OF ARIZONA, 3rd Edition, Univ. Arizona Press, Tucson, 1969

Benson, Lyman, THE NATIVE CACTI OF CALIFORNIA, Stanford Univ. Press, Stanford, California, 1969

Benson, Lyman, Cactaceae in Correll, D. S., and M. C. Johnson, MANUAL OF THE VASCULAR PLANTS OF TEXAS, Texas Research Foundation, Benner, Texas, 1970

Borg, John, CACTI, 4th Edition, Blanford Press, London, 1970

Britton, N. L., and J. N. Rose, THE CACTACEAE (4 Vols.), Carnegie Institution of Washington, D. C., 1919-1923

Cactus and Succulent Journal (44 Vols.), The Cactus and Succulent Society of America, 132 West Union Street, Pasadena, California, 1929-1972

Carlson, Raymond, THE FLOWERING CACTUS, McGraw-Hill Book Co., New York, 1954

Chidamian, Claude, THE BOOK OF CACTI AND OTHER SUCCULENTS, American Garden Guild and Doubleday & Co., Garden City, New York, 1958.

Craig, R. T., MAMMILLARIA HANDBOOK, Abbey Garden Press, Pasadena, California, 1945

Cutak, Ladislaus, CACTUS GUIDE, D. Van Nostrand Co., Princeton, New Jersey, 1956

Haage, Walther, CACTI AND SUCCULENTS, E. P. Dutton & Co., New York, 1963

Hadley, Neil F., "Desert species and adaptation," American Scientist 60 (3):338-347, 1972

Haselton, Scott E., EPIPHYLLUM HANDBOOK, Abbey Garden Press, Pasadena, California, 1946

Morton, Julia F., "Cadushi (Cereus repandus Mill.) A useful cactus of Curacao," Economic Botany 21 (2):185-191, 1967

Schultes, Richard E., "The plant kingdom and hallucinogens" (Part III), Bulletin on Narcotics 22 (1):28-56, 1970

Schumann, Karl, GESAMTBESCHREIBUNG DER KAKTEEN, Verlag von J. Neumann, Neudamm, 1898, NACHTRAGE, 1903

Subik, Rudolf, CACTI AND SUCCULENTS, Hamlyn Publ. Co., New York, 1968

Thornber, John J., and Frances Bonker, THE FANTASTIC CLAN, Macmillan Co., New York, 1932

Weniger, Del, CACTI OF THE SOUTHWEST, Univ. Texas Press, Austin, 1970

MEASURING SCALE (IN 10THS OF AN INCH)

G